OLYSLAGER AUTO LIBRARY

# American Cars of the 1930s

compiled by the OLYSLAGER ORGANISATION
edited by Bart H. Vanderveen

FREDERICK WARNE & Co Ltd
London and New York

Library of Congress Catalog Card Number 72-91870

ISBN 0 7232 1266X

Filmset by Keyspools Ltd, Golborne, Lancs
Printed in Great Britain by Cox & Wyman Ltd, Fakenham

# INTRODUCTION

This 'picture album' deals with American cars of the period 1930 to 1939. The emphasis is on the popular models of the 'Big Three', namely General Motors, Ford and Chrysler, and the largest 'independents' such as Hudson, Nash, Packard and Studebaker, rather than the more glamorous 'classics' such as Cord, Duesenberg, Marmon and Pierce Arrow. The intention is firstly to present a review of this important decade of American automotive production, during which time square box-shaped body styles gave way to streamlined notch- and fast-back styling, and secondly to provide a handy reference work which serves as a means of identifying the various cars by make and model year.

Many of these 'American' cars were actually produced outside the United States, for a variety of reasons. Several popular types were assembled or manufactured (or partly manufactured) in Canada, where assembly and manufacturing plants had been set up, mainly in Ontario, because it was reasonably close to Detroit. In addition to supplying home-market customers, these Canadian products were marketed in Britain and throughout the Commonwealth. Export to these countries was usually in CKD (completely knocked down) or PKD (partly knocked down) form, final assembly and again part-manufacturing usually taking place in the country of destination. In the process there was plenty of opportunity to 'tailor' certain types of cars for a particular market, not only by fitting, for example, small-bore engines in order to meet (or bend!) local horsepower taxation regulations but also by changing marque names. For example: the Plymouth, Chrysler's cheapest range of cars, was marketed in Britain under the Chrysler name, which was the Chrysler Corporation's top-line marque. This process became popularly known as 'badge engineering' and still takes place. Sometimes of course this is done because a certain marque may already have been registered by another manufacturer. Many cars and CKD packs were also exported direct from the United States to distributors and assembly plants in various countries in Europe, Asia, Africa, South America etc.

An important point to remember when reviewing American cars (whether of US or Canadian origin) is that 'model years' are different from 'calendar years' and as such were not always strictly adhered to by distributors in overseas markets. If, for example, in a certain export market a surplus of a certain type of American car occurred at the end of the 'model year' (often as early as August-September) the distributor would continue selling it, even into the next calendar year, with the result that it would be registered in the year following its 'model year'. Invariably such left-over stock of the previous year's models would be sold at attractive 'clearance' prices.

American autos of the nineteen thirties were extremely popular all over the world and their ruggedness, combined with powerful engines, spacious bodies and competitive prices, made them particularly attractive in many overseas countries where large-scale motorisation was still in its infancy. Henry Ford's 'Tin Lizzy' Model T had of course been instrumental in creating much goodwill for American cars and his successive A, B and V8 models could be found in the most distant corners of the globe. The enormous competition from General Motors, Chrysler and the rest proved to be of great benefit to potential buyers.

The following pages have been laid out on a year-by-year basis and, as far as possible, each make appears in alphabetical order under the section relating to its particular year for easy reference. Obviously the book is not a complete survey but it is thought to be sufficiently comprehensive to meet the need for a work of this kind. The models included could be divided into three categories, namely USA domestic production (with standard or custom bodywork), models assembled/produced in other countries, and exported chassis with 'foreign' bodywork. As a result there are probably some 'American' car types which may never have 'set tyre' on American soil.

**Piet Olyslager** MSIA, MSAE, KIVI

## 1930

During 1930 the American automotive industry produced 2,784,745 passenger cars and 571,241 trucks and buses. This figure (about twice the number of vehicles taxed in Great Britain) compared very unfavourably with 1929 which had shown figures of 4,587,400 and 771,020 respectively. The reason was that America as well as much of the rest of the world lay deep in an economic crisis. The Wall Street crash of the previous year had caused a slump which also affected Europe and the British Commonwealth and meant, or was going to mean, the end of many a car manufacturer. Other US statistics for 1930 (the 1929 figures are given in brackets) show that there were some 341,000 (471,000) automobile workers and 48,658 (52,588) motor vehicle dealers. The wholesale value of cars, trucks and buses produced amounted to $2,035 (3,413) million. The total number of US vehicle registrations was 26,545,000 (26,501,000) of which slightly under 3·5 (3·4) million were trucks and buses. On the technical side, most 1930 US cars had flat-base wheels with tyre sizes varying from 20 to 18 in. and double-bar bumpers, usually with a rounded profile. Mechanical fuel pumps had begun to replace the vacuum tank type fuel feed system.

---

4A: **Buick Six,** built in Canada (McLaughlin). Last year of six-cylinder Buicks. Three Series: 40, 50 and 60.
4B: **Cadillac Series 353 V8** Cabriolet Imperial by Fleetwood. V12 and V16 models and hydraulic valve lifters made their appearance.
4C: **Chevrolet Universal Series AD** Coach. 'Stovebolt Six' ohv engine had replaced four-cylinder for 1929 model year. Body by Fisher.
4D: **Chrysler 77 Six** had 4340-cc 93-bhp engine. Shown here is Canadian-built rhd export model with 27·3 HP (RAC) rating.

HX 9469
4A Buick

4D Chrysler

4C Chevrolet

3955
FLEETWOOD
4B Cadillac

5A: **Cord L29** bristled with unconventional design and engineering features such as front-wheel drive and double $\frac{1}{4}$-elliptic springs.
5B: **Cord L29 Brougham** was first introduced in 1929 and was powered by eight-cylinder 125-bhp Lycoming engine. Continued until 1932.
5C: **DeSoto CK Six.** This make was introduced by Chrysler in 1928 to fill the gap between Plymouth and Dodge. Shown is $875 Sedan.
5D: **Dodge DH Six** Sedan, powered by 189·8-cu in. L-head engine with 5·2:1 compression ratio developing 60 bhp at 3400 rpm.
5E: **Dodge DC Eight** Sedan. This was Dodge Brothers' first eight-cylinder. Output was 75 bhp, cubic capacity 220·7 cu in.

5A Cord

5B Cord

5C DeSoto

5D Dodge

5E Dodge

## 1930

6A: **Essex Super Six Challenger** Phaeton as marketed in Great Britain by Hudson Essex Motors Ltd of Chiswick, W. 4, at £245. Photo taken on the roof of the Chiswick premises.
6B: **Essex Super Six Challenger** Coupé. Styling, with dicky seat, was typical of the period. Engine was 2638-cc L-head of 18·2 HP (RAC). Essex was lower-price model range of Hudson Motor Co.
6C: **Ford Model A** had 103½-in. wb and in the US there were sixteen body styles. This Convertible Coupé model has survived in England. Roadster version looked rather similar but had folding windshield (screen).
6D: **Ford Model A** Special Convertible coachwork by Schutter & van Bakel of Amsterdam, Netherlands. 35 of these were produced in 1930–31 for Amsterdam Ford dealer. Nearly 4·5 million Model As were produced from late 1927 until early 1932.

6A Essex

6B Essex

MY 5302

6C Ford

6D Ford

7A: **Hudson Super Eight** Roadster on short-wheelbase chassis. One of ten body styles on two chassis lengths (wb 119 and 126 in.). Windshield could be opened, or folded flat completely.
7B: **Hudson Super Eight.** Front view of Roadster. Double-bar front bumper was typical of 1929–31 American cars. Note large headlamps. Colours: 'cheerfully smart, or subdued and dignified, as you prefer'.
7C: **Hudson Super Eight** Brougham on long-wheelbase chassis. Fabric-covered rear-quarter panels and 'Landau Arms'. Wire wheels and two spares were optional. (Standard: wood wheels, one spare rim, five tyres).
7D: **LaSalle Series 340 V8** Seven-passenger Sedan. LaSalle was introduced by Cadillac in 1927 to enter the medium-price market. 1930 models had 90-bhp V8 engine. Coachwork by Fisher.

7A Hudson

7B Hudson

7C Hudson

7D LaSalle

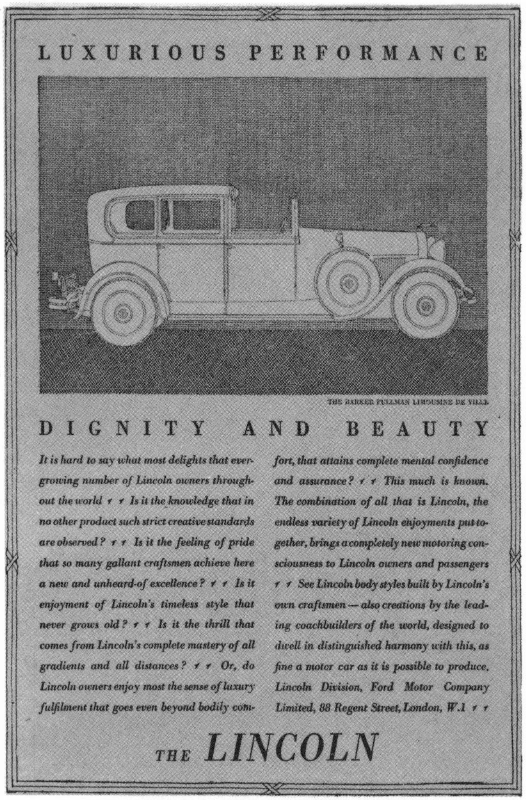
LUXURIOUS PERFORMANCE
THE BARKER PULLMAN LIMOUSINE DE VILLE
DIGNITY AND BEAUTY
It is hard to say what most delights that ever-growing number of Lincoln owners throughout the world ❦ ❦ Is it the knowledge that in no other product such strict creative standards are observed? ❦ ❦ Is it the feeling of pride that so many gallant craftsmen achieve here a new and unheard-of excellence? ❦ ❦ Is it enjoyment of Lincoln's timeless style that never grows old? ❦ ❦ Is it the thrill that comes from Lincoln's complete mastery of all gradients and all distances? ❦ ❦ Or, do Lincoln owners enjoy most the sense of luxury fulfilment that goes even beyond bodily comfort, that attains complete mental confidence and assurance? ❦ ❦ This much is known. The combination of all that is Lincoln, the endless variety of Lincoln enjoyments put together, brings a completely new motoring consciousness to Lincoln owners and passengers ❦ ❦ See Lincoln body styles built by Lincoln's own craftsmen — also creations by the leading coachbuilders of the world, designed to dwell in distinguished harmony with this, as fine a motor car as it is possible to produce. Lincoln Division, Ford Motor Company Limited, 88 Regent Street, London, W.1 ❦ ❦
THE LINCOLN

8A Lincoln

8A: **Lincoln V8.** Period advertisement (July 1930) showing Barker Pullman Limousine DeVille, one of many special body styles available on this top-line chassis of the Ford Motor Co.
8B: **Marquette Series 30** was Buick's cheapest range. There were six models, all with 114-in. wb, ranging from Business Coupé (Model 36) at $990 to four-door Sedan (Model 37) at $1060.
8C: **Nash Eight.** In 1930 Nash Motors introduced an eight-cylinder engine. Sedan shown was converted for running on paraffin in Holland when petrol was rationed (c. 1946).
8D: **Oldsmobile F30 Six** Sedan, shown here with disc wheels, priced just under $1000 in 1929/30. Oldsmobile also offered a smart but short-lived luxury V8 model named Viking.

8B Marquette

GZ-31610

8C Nash

8D Oldsmobile

9A: **Packard Custom Eight, Seventh Series, Model 740.** Special Dutch coachwork by Schutter & van Bakel of Amsterdam. Spotlight at front was manually operated from driver's seat. Note disc wheels and large luggage compartment at rear. Also known as 'Big Eight'. Engine had $3\frac{1}{2} \times 5$ in. bore and stroke and developed 106 bhp. Wheelbase $140\frac{1}{2}$ in. Companion model was DeLuxe Eight (wb $145\frac{1}{2}$ in.); both were in production for one year from August 1929.
9B: **Packard Standard Eight, Seventh Series, Model 733** Phaeton. One of ten body styles available on this $134\frac{1}{2}$-in. wb chassis, which was in production from 20 August 1929 until 14 August 1930. Prices varied from $2425 for 401 Phaeton and 402 Roadster to to $2775 for 405 Limousine. A companion model on $127\frac{1}{2}$-in. wb chassis was the Model 726 which, however, was only available with one body style (403 Sedan, $2375). Prices shown are those at time of introduction.

H-31620
Schutter & van Bakel

9A Packard

9B Packard

## 1930

10A: **Plymouth 30U Four** Sedan. Chrysler Corporation's low-price make, introduced in 1928. In spite of the stock market crash of 1929, Plymouth sales in the USA boomed, especially when in 1930 all Chrysler, DeSoto and Dodge dealers were given Plymouth franchises.
10B: **Pontiac 6-30B Six** Sedan sold at $825 and differed from 1929 model mainly by way of a new slanting windshield and improved brakes. Originally a companion car to the Oakland, the more popular Pontiac soon went ahead of Oakland and in 1931 the latter was discontinued.

10A Plymouth

10B Pontiac

This was another bad sales year for the American motor industry and model changes were minimal. Due to the nationwide economic illness, following the Great Depression, sales of cars and trucks took another dive to 1,973,090 and 416,648 respectively. During the year the 50 millionth US motor vehicle was produced, but at the year's end the number of motor vehicle dealers had dwindled to under 44,000 (there were 52,588 in 1929) and the total number of vehicle registrations had dropped to 2,390,000. Many manufacturers had available large and luxurious models of the type the public had indicated it wanted until the Great Depression came, and these powerful cars were now offered at reduced prices. Many manufacturers introduced refinements such as free-wheeling (available on some 15 makes) and synchromesh transmissions. Hydraulic brakes were still reserved for the more expensive cars. Among the few new makes introduced in 1931 were Studebaker's Rockne and the DeVaux. Both were short-lived. The latter was launched in January in Grand Rapids, Michigan, and looked quite promising. However, after 14 months the company got into financial difficulty and was taken over by Continental, the engine makers, who continued it under their own name (models: Beacon, Flyer, Red Seal) until 1934.

11A Auburn

11A: **Auburn 898 Eight.** There were two basic models, the Standard 898 and the 898A Custom series, each with seven body styles.
11B: **Buick Eight Series 50.** Cheapest Sedan in Buick's 1931 range was this Model 50 two-door ($1035); costliest was 90L ($2035).
11C: **Cadillac Series 452A V16** Transformable Town Brougham by Fleetwood. Wheelbase 148 in. List price of a typical Cadillac V16: $5950.

11B Buick

FLEETWOOD

11C Cadillac

AM-86-89

12A Chevrolet

FSA 425D

12B Chevrolet

**Chevrolet Independence Series AE**
Mechanically, the 1931 Chevrolets were not much different from the 1930 models but wb was 2 in. longer (109 in.) and most of the bodywork was restyled. There were 14 models using this chassis and in addition a Sedan Delivery (van) and three commercial chassis options. The straight black-enamel headlamp tiebar was replaced by a curved chrome-plated one and there were more louvres in the hood (bonnet). Shown here are:
12A: Convertible Cabriolet. This car has survived in Czechoslovakia and is in regular use.
12B: Right-hand drive Phaeton, surviving in England. Note folding windshield.
12C: Special Town Sedan with open front compartment and Roadster windshield.
12D: Three-window Coupé DeLuxe with grille in front of radiator shell.

12C Chevrolet

12D Chevrolet

13A: **Chrysler Imperial Custom Eight** was new in 1931 and superbly elegant. It had a 384-cu in. engine, developing 125 bhp. The chassis was used by various makers of luxury coachwork.
13B: **DeSoto CF Eight** was the last of the straight-eights built by this division of the Chrysler Corporation. It developed 77 bhp and wb of the Sedan shown was 114 in.
13C: **Dodge Brothers** period advertisement. The Company had been founded by John and Horace Dodge in 1914 and became part of the Chrysler Corporation in 1928. The word 'dependability' was first used by Dodge.

13A Chrysler

13B DeSoto

DODGE DEPENDABILITY
NEW DODGE SIX SEDAN $845
New Beauty AND THE DEPENDABILITY FOR WHICH DODGE IS FAMED
You naturally expect that Dodge, having earned a world-wide reputation for dependability, should prize that reputation. And Dodge does prize it. » » The beautiful New Dodge Six and Eight are exactly the kind of car you would expect Dodge to build. » » With all of their new smartness and luxury, they hold fast to every Dodge principle of excellence. They carry still higher a fine tradition for cars of long life, outstanding economy and dependability. » » The New Dodge Six and Eight are larger, finer, faster, smoother and more comfortable. Yet they remain at traditional Dodge price-levels. » » Today, more than ever before, it is important to buy a car that will cost little to run during a long period of life. And never before have Dodge cars embodied so much that guarantees satisfaction and economy through years of service.
Carrying on a Fine Tradition: LONGER WHEELBASES give gracious riding comfort and smart, fleet appearance—DOUBLE-DROP FRAME, box-type, providing low-swung grace and great strength of chassis—ADVANCED PERFORMANCE from engines of larger size and greater efficiency—MONO-PIECE STEEL BODIES, insulated, jointless and squeakless, extremely strong, with Bedford Cord upholstery and other fine appointments—INTERNAL HYDRAULIC BRAKES, safe, weatherproof, positive, self-equalizing—WIRE WHEELS, five wire wheels at no extra cost.
© 1931 by Dodge Brothers Corporation
New Dodge Six $815 to $845, New Dodge Eight $1095 to $1135; Standard Six $735 to $835, Standard Eight $995 to $1095. F.O.B. Factory

13C Dodge

14A: **Essex Super Six Challenger** Sedan was quite popular in Great Britain where it sold at £225. Engine was 2368-cc L-head, rated at 18·2 HP (RAC). Wire wheels were optional extra.
14B: **Ford Model A** Coupé (Type 45B) was one of 18 body styles available. In Britain there was also the Model AF which had reduced-bore 2-litre 14·9 HP (treasury rating) engine.
14C: **Ford Model A** Panel Delivery DeLuxe (Type 130B) was based on the $103\frac{1}{2}$-in. wb car chassis and was one of over 60 commercial and truck models offered in the 1931 catalogue.
14D: **Ford Model A** Phaeton (Type 35B), used by the (British) Indian army as a staff car. In April 1931 the 20 millionth Ford was produced and a V8 engine was under way.

HX 4194
14A Essex

14B Ford

14C Ford

14D Ford

15A: **Hudson Great Eight** seven-passenger Sedan. This luxurious model was built on a 126-in. wb and featured adjustable front and rear seats (which could also be cranked vertically) and hydraulic shock absorbers which could be controlled for ride comfort from the driver's seat. Engine cubic capacity was 3½ litres.
15B: **LaSalle V8** Convertible Coupé on Series 345A chassis. Engine produced 95 bhp at 3400 rpm. LaSalle cars were produced by Cadillac from 1927 until 1940 and were 'lower-priced carbon copies of the Caddy'. Model shown had 134-in. wb, resulting in long 'rear deck'. Prices started at about $2295.
15C: **Lincoln V8** Sport Phaeton, one of various types available. In addition to factory-built bodies this high-grade chassis was available with the work of well-known coachbuilders such as Dietrich and Waterhouse. Lincoln was founded in 1920 and became a division of the Ford Motor Co. in 1922. Model shown had 145-in. wb and 120-bhp engine.

La Salle

15B LaSalle

15A Hudson

15C Lincoln

16A: **Oldsmobile F31 Six** Sedan. 1931 Oldsmobiles had synchromesh gearbox and downdraught carburettor for the first time. Note light-coloured spokes of wood wheels. Fisher bodywork was similar to that used for other General Motors products—Chevrolet and Pontiac. Oldsmobile was founded as early as 1896 and taken over by General Motors in 1909.

16B: **Packard Standard Eight, Eighth Series, Model 833** Sedan. This seven-seater had a $134\frac{1}{2}$-in. wb and carried body style number 464. The Model 833 series (11 body styles) and its $127\frac{1}{2}$-in. wb companion Model 826 (Sedan only) were in production from August 1930 until June 1931. Engine developed 100 bhp.

16C: **Plymouth PA Four** Coupé had $109\frac{3}{8}$-in. wb and 196-cu in. engine developing 56 bhp. Sales of Plymouth cars soared to 109,487 during this generally bad Depression year in which several car manufacturers went bankrupt. There were also two- and four-door Sedan, Business Coupé and Roadster, Roadster with Dickey, and Convertible Phaeton body styles.

16B Packard

16A Oldsmobile

16C Plymouth

17A: **Pontiac 401 Six** shared Fisher bodywork with Chevrolet and Oldsmobile (qv). This now rare Coupé has survived in England. Oakland, Pontiac's 'father', was formed in 1907 and two years later became part of the General Motors Corporation. Pontiac was a lower-price offshoot introduced in 1926, but it rapidly overshadowed the Oakland range which during 1931 was retained as a V8 but was then dropped altogether.
17B: **Pontiac 401 Six** looked much like contemporary Chevrolet, except for radiator grille. Engine was L-head with $3\frac{5}{16}$ x $3\frac{7}{8}$ in. bore and stroke (200 cu in.). Complete model range consisted of three Coupés (Standard, Sport and Convertible) and three Sedans (two-door as shown, Standard four-door and Custom). Wheelbase 112 in. Oakland range similar but 251-cu in. V8 engine (B x S $3\frac{7}{16}$ x $3\frac{3}{8}$ in.) and 117-in. wb.

17C: **Reo 8-35 Custom Royale Eight** Coupé. This 5·9-litre car was a luxury companion car to the well-known Flying Cloud. It was styled by Count Alexis de Sakhnoffsky and featured automatic chassis lubrication. Reo derived its name from the initials of Ransom Eli Olds, who had founded Oldsmobile in 1896 and who left in 1904 to start the Reo Motor Car Co.

17B Pontiac

AAV 80

17A Pontiac

17C Reo

1932 opened in the gloomy economic climate of a deepening depression. With the market now 'deader than a doornail' this promised to be the worst year since 1918. Total US production was 1,135,491 cars and 235,187 trucks, a drop of over one million compared with the previous year. Many manufacturers saw their production cut by about half, yet one or two others were not doing too badly. Miraculously, Plymouth production and sales actually increased. Chrysler could claim that its Plymouth was the only car in the industry whose sales rose in 1932 (124,777 vs 109,487). Styling-wise, 1932 was an interesting year with more curves, single bumper bars and drop-centre wheels. Full-skirted fenders made their first appearance (on the Graham), and free-wheels and vacuum-actuated clutches were fashionable. Inside sun visors replaced the familiar exterior shades for improved looks and reduced wind resistance. Production of carburettors, now increasingly of the downdraft type, was more and more monopolised by a few mass-producers; the smaller manufacturers were on the way out. Biggest automotive news of the year was undoubtedly Ford's introduction of a new model with V8 engine, replacing the popular four-cylinder Model A.

18A: **Buick Eight 90** with Cabriolet Coupé coachwork by Vanden Plas of Brussels, Belgium. The Series 90 had a 134-in. wb.
18B: **Buick Eight** Convertible Phaeton, factory-built bodywork available on Series 50,60 and 90 chassis (wb 114 ¾, 118 and 134 in. respectively).
18C: **Cadillac Series 355B V8** Town Sedan. Features offered included full-range ride regulator (suspension adjustment control). Also V12 and V16 models.
18D: **Chevrolet Confederate Series BA** DeLuxe Sport Roadster. First Chevrolet with built-in radiator grille. DeLuxe had chromed doors in hood.

18A Buick

18B Buick

18C Cadillac

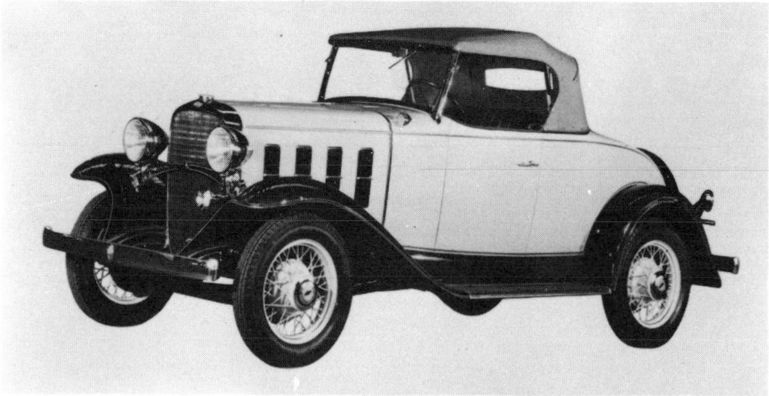
18D Chevrolet

19A: **Chrysler CG Imperial Custom Eight** chassis was long (wb 145 in.) and majestic. It was used by various craftsmen/coachbuilders. This double-cowl Phaeton (design LeBaron) was built by Briggs.
19B: **DeSoto SD Six** Sedan. Along with the other Chrysler Corporation cars the 1932 DeSotos had 'Floating Power' rubber engine mountings and optional free-wheel behind gearbox.
19C: **Dodge DM Four** Sedan. For the first time since 1928 there was a Dodge Four again. The L-head engine had 92·1 x 120·7 mm bore and stroke, and developed 65 bhp. Phaeton also available.
19D: **Dodge DK Eight** Sedan. Engine output 100 bhp. 1932 saw introduction of Dodge 'Ram' trademark as radiator cap ornament. This was the last of the Dodge straight-eights. Wheelbase $122\frac{3}{8}$ in.

19A Chrysler

19B DeSoto

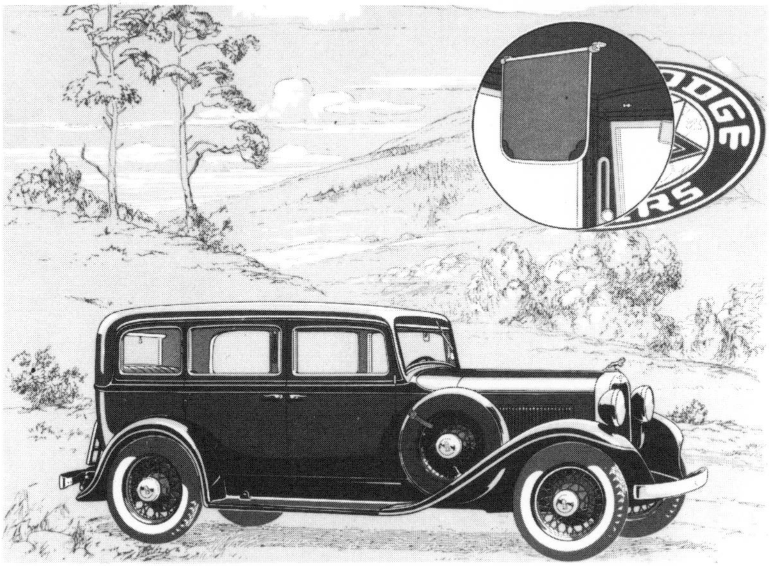
19C Dodge

19D Dodge

**Ford Model 18 V8** was introduced 9th March 1932, following nearly 4,500,000 Model As. Four-cylinder engine remained available in virtually the same auto, designated **Model B.** The V8, which produced 65 bhp at 3400 rpm, could be seen as Ford's answer to Chevrolet's Six and was an instant success. There were 14 body styles (not counting the B commercials), some of which are shown here:

20A: British Model B Fordor 24 HP was also available as BF Fourteen-Nine (14·9 HP). Resembled Model 18 except for V8 ornaments. Built until 1935.

20B: Model 18 Cabriolet (Type 68) Note V8 ornaments on wheel hub caps and headlamp tiebar. Wheelbase 106 in.

20C: Model 18 Cabriolet with top down and dickey (or rumble) seat opened up. Speed up to 75 mph.

20D: Model B Standard Coupé (Type 45) with 50-bhp four-cylinder engine. V8 engine and dickey seat optional.

20A Ford

20C Ford

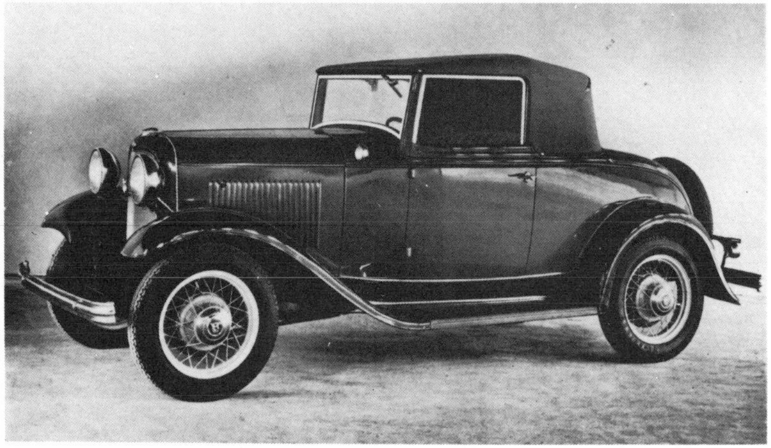

20B Ford

20D Ford

21A: **Hudson's Essex Terraplane** replaced earlier Essex range.in July. Famous woman pilot Amelia Earhart came to Hudson Motor Car Co. for its christening. Prices started at a low $425.

21B: **Hudson Special.** Six of these vehicles were built for the Japanese Government for military use in Manchuria. Only the rearmost wheels were driven. The spares were idler/support wheels.

21C: **LaSalle Series 345B V8** Victoria Coupé. Body by Fisher. Wheelbase was 136 in. Due to the Depression, Cadillac and LaSalle sales dropped to 8,085 from 29,781 in 1931.

21D: **Lincoln KB V12** was new in 1932 when V8 was discontinued. 145-in. wb chassis was used for a variety of special bodies. Next Lincoln V8s were 9EL and 9EH Cosmopolitan in 1949.

21A Hudson

21B Hudson

La Salle

21C LaSalle

21D Lincoln

22A: **Marmon V16** Convertible Sedan. The 9·1-litre engine was designed by Colonel Howard Marmon and incorporated wide use of aluminium alloy. It was first introduced in 1931 at $4925 for the complete car. British prices: chassis £1,295, complete £1,625.
22B: **Nash Standard Eight 1070** Sedan. This 121-in. wb model was one of the 1932 2nd Series, introduced in mid-year. Other models in this Series were the Big Six (116-in. wb), Special Eight (128-in.), Advanced Eight (133-in.) and Ambassador Eight (142-in.).
22C: **Oldsmobile L32 Eight** was new for 1932 and resembled the F32 Six in appearance. Shown is the Coach (two-door Sedan) with standard Fisher bodywork. Spare wheel mounting was either at rear, as shown, or in fender well.

AK-90-90
22B Nash

22A Marmon

22C Oldsmobile

23A: **Packard Eight DeLuxe, Ninth Series, Model 904** Coupé by Dietrich, formally known as 'Individual Custom Stationary Coupé', Body Model No. 2068. Ninth Series was produced from June 1931 to January 1933.
23B: **Pierce-Arrow Eight** Sedan with characteristic streamlined headlamps. Company was under control of Studebaker and built eight- and twelve-cylinder models. The V-12 came in $5\frac{1}{2}$- and 7-litre forms, developing up to 175 bhp.
23C: **Pontiac 402 Six** Coach. For 1932 the Oakland was dropped and the Pontiac came as either a Six or Eight. Wheelbase was 114 and 117 in. respectively. Six body styles.

23A Packard

23B Pierce-Arrow

23C Pontiac

24A Rockne

24B Studebaker

24A: **Rockne Six 65** Coupé was produced by Studebaker through its subsidiary the Rockne Motor Corporation which in 1931 was formed to sell low-price cars. Rockne sold well (better than all other Studebaker products) but not enough and the line was discontinued in 1933 Named after football coach Knute Rockne.
24B: **Studebaker President Eight** seven-passenger Limousine was top-line model on 130-in. wb and powered by 5½-litre engine. Studebaker's other Eight was the Commander Series on 125-in. wb. Studebaker had started in 1852 and in 1902 had made its first (electric) car. Like most other firms it suffered badly from the Depression.
24C: **Willys-Knight Six** was Willys-Overland's last car with sleeve-valve engine. Shown is the model 66E Sedan which cost $1395. Later in the year the small and cheap Willys 77 was introduced but sales were extremely bad, mainly due to the Depression. Willys' earlier cheap car, the Whippet, had been discontinued in 1931.

24C Willys

25A Buick

OY 5518

25B Buick

25C Cadillac

The year 1933 saw almost universal adoption of V-shaped radiator grilles, slanted windshields and other forms of streamlining. Among the technical 'novelties' were independent front suspension, valve seat inserts, reflex glass tail- and stop-lights, 'No-Draft Ventilation' with swivelling vent-windows (Fisher Bodies), use of accelerator pedal for starting and power-assisted brakes. Reo was the first with an automatic transmission. It was not a sophisticated affair, featuring only two forward ratios (Low and Direct) without the possibility of detent down shift ('kick down') but, with its big engine producing 'bags of torque' it provided effortless and sensational driving. Statistically, too, things looked a bit brighter. Car production was up by 438,021 to 1,573,512, trucks and buses by 111,358 to 346.545. The wholesale value of these 1,920,057 vehicles was $949 million, but another 4105 motor dealers had gone out of business and total car registrations were also down. Truck and bus registrations, however, were slightly up. It was about this time that White introduced its 'pancake' truck engine with twelve horizontally opposed cylinders. Ralph de Palma celebrated his 25th anniversary as a racer and Louis Meyer, driving a Miller, won the Indianapolis Sweepstakes at an average speed of 104·162 mph.

---

25A: **Buick Eight** with German Convertible coachwork built by Alexis Kellner of Heilbronn a/Neckar. First year with 'knee action' ifs.
25B: **Buick Eight Series CA** with right-hand drive, built by General Motors of Canada Ltd as McLaughlin-Buick, for British market.
25C: **Cadillac Series 355C V8** Limousine featured no-draft ventilation. Wheelbase was 140 in. and prices started at $2895. V-shaped radiator grille.
25D: **Chevrolet Master Series CA** Coupé. Standard CC had louvres in hood and shorter wb (107 vs 110 in.). Master CA was first known as Eagle.

25D Chevrolet

26A: **Chrysler CL Custom Imperial Eight** with typical double-cowl Phaeton bodywork. Power output was 135 bhp with 5·8:1 or 125 bhp with 5·2:1 compression ratio, both at 3200 rpm. Bore and stroke were no less than $3\frac{1}{2} \times 5$ in. giving 384·8-cu in. piston displacement.
26B: **Chrysler CT Royal Eight** Sedan (top) and **Chrysler CO Six** Brougham sold at $995 and $795 respectively. There were four other body styles in the Eight series, five others in the Six.
26C: **DeSoto SD Special Six** Brougham had split windshield and forward-opening doors. The engine was the familiar L-head and in this application had $3\frac{1}{4} \times 4\frac{3}{8}$ in. bore and stroke resulting in a cubic capacity of 217·7 cu in. Wheelbase was 114 in.
26D: **Dodge DP Six** Sedan was not unlike the DeSoto but had $3\frac{1}{8}$ in. bore engine (201·3 cu in.). It was also available with eight-cylinder engine, as Model DO, with 282·1-cu in. capacity and maximum output of 100 bhp. Wheelbase 115 and 122 in.

26B Chrysler

26C DeSoto

26A Chrysler

26D Dodge

AXB 701

27A Essex

27B Ford

27C Ford

27D Hudson

27A: **Essex** became **Terraplane** in 1933 (1934 in Britain). In Britain the name **Essex Terraplane** was used in 1933. Shown is **Terraplane Eight** Convertible Coupé.

27B: **Ford Model 40 V8** with Swiss Convertible bodywork. The Model 40 was also available with the old four-cylinder engine. Wheelbase was 112 in.

27C: **Ford Model 40 V8** Tudor Sedan (Body Type 700) was one of many body styles offered by the factory. The four-cylinder was similar except for V8 ornaments.

27D: **Hudson L Major Eight Brougham** was the luxurious model. Hudson's bread-and-butter lines were the popular Super Six and Essex Terraplanes (Six and Eight).

28A: **Hupmobile 322F Eight** Convertible Coupé had eight-in-line engine and 122-in. wb chassis. It was produced by the Hupp Motor Car Corp. which existed from 1908 until 1941.
28B: **LaSalle Series 345C V8** Sedan had the same 353-cu in. engine as Cadillac Series 355C. Like most American 1933 models it had 'skirted' front fenders (wings). Wheelbase was 136 in.
28C: **Lincoln KB V12** with Convertible bodywork. Two chassis lengths were available: 136 in. (KA, 2nd Series) and 145 in. (KB). The latter chassis was frequently used by custom body builders.
28D: **Nash Big Six 1127** Town Sedan was one of six body styles available. Engine was L-head with $3\frac{1}{4} \times 4\frac{3}{8}$ in. bore and stroke. Wheelbase 116 in. Also with 8-cyl. engine.

28A Hupmobile

28B LaSalle

28C Lincoln

28D Nash

29A: **Oldsmobile F33 Six** Sedan shared Fisher body styling with other General Motors products. The L33 Eight had similar bodywork with the exception of the radiator grille which had slanted bars and a different ornament on top. The cubic capacity of the two engines was 221·4 and 240·3 cu in. respectively.

29B: **Packard Eight, Tenth Series, Model 1002** Sedan. This series (Jan. to Aug. 1933) also comprised Super Eight Models 1003 and 1004 and Twelve Models 1005 and 1006. The Eight had two wb sizes—127½ in. (1001) and 136 in. (1002, shown). Altogether Packard listed 55 body styles for the Tenth Series.

29C: **Pierce-Arrow 'Silver Arrow' V12** Sedan, one of five made by hand and offered at $10,000 at Chicago World's Fair and New York Auto Show. Engine developed 175 bhp and spare wheels were in lockers behind front wheels. Note advanced styling and absence of running boards.

29B Packard

29A Oldsmobile

29C Pierce-Arrow

30A: **Plymouth PD Six** was claimed to be the 'largest six in the low-price field'. Chrysler's Plymouth concept had been well received by the public and sales were phenomenal.
30B: **Plymouth** alias **Fargo.** Chrysler's fleet and government sales being handled by the Fargo Division, Plymouth cars for the US Army and Civilian Conservation Corps were officially known as Fargos.
30C: **Pontiac 601 Eight.** In 1933 Pontiac offered only eight-cylinder models. The engine was an in-line L-head with $3\frac{3}{16} \times 3\frac{1}{2}$ in. bore and stroke, giving 223·4 cu in. piston displacement.
30D: **Pontiac 601 Eight** two-door Sedan or Coach. Other body styles included Standard, Sport and Convertible Coupés, Roadster, Four-door and Touring Sedan. Wheelbase for all models was 115 in.

30A Plymouth

30B Plymouth

30C Pontiac

30D Pontiac

31A: **Rockne Six 65** was low-price 110-in. wb car offered by Studebaker. It sold well, both at home and in various export markets, in Coupé, Phaeton and Sedan (shown) form. Over 30,000 were made, selling at prices from $585 to $675.
31B: **Studebaker President Eight** Sedan used as a baker's van in the Netherlands in about 1943. Like so many cars in war-torn Europe it was converted to run on producer gas and this particular installation was rather cumbersome.
31C: **Willys Four 77** Coupé was light, cheap and not exactly elegant but sold well enough to save Willys-Overland from bankruptcy. Engine was 134-cu in. 45-bhp. A Six Model 99 was also available (213·3 cu in. 80 bhp) but not for long.

-60120
31B Studebaker

31A Rockne

31C Willys

32A Buick

1934 saw more streamlining and increased use of independent front suspensions. Chevrolet produced its 10 millionth car to celebrate its 23rd anniversary and nation-wide automotive production was definitely on the upswing with 2,177,919 cars and 575,192 trucks and buses. Wholesale value of replacement parts and accessories produced during this year amounted to $299,879,633—a 28% increase over 1933. The millionth Plymouth and Nash were produced (since 1928 and 1917 respectively) and world-wide Ford production during the year reached 859,526. Chrysler and DeSoto introduced the revolutionary but ill-fated 'Airflow' design with 'interlocked' body and frame and automatic Overdrive, and Graham offered a supercharged engine. Cadillac pioneered and first used a generator with controlled current to keep the battery fully charged at all times for extra loads (radio, heater). Hudson was first to introduce pinned piston rings in American cars and offered luggage compartment with concealed tyre at rear. Studebaker was the first manufacturer to use lead bronze con rod bearings and was the last to produce a Six with firing order 1–4–2–6–3–5; thereafter 1–5–3–6–2–4 became universal. Nash introduced the lower-price LaFayette car, and 'Wild Bill' Cummings averaged 104·865 mph to win Indianapolis Sweepstakes.

---

32A: **Buick Eight Series 90** Club Sedan with built-in trunk, Model 91 had 136-in. wb, weighed 4980 pounds and cost $1965. It was one of an entirely new range of Buicks.
32B: **Buick Eight Series 60** Sedan, Model 67, had 128-in. wb and sold at $1425. Other Series were 40 (117-in. wb) and 50 (119-in. wb) Lowest-priced Buick was model 46 Coupé at $795.
32C: **Cadillac Series 20 V8** Seven-passenger Sedan and Imperial Sedan had 136-in. wb and shared same Fisher bodywork. Spare wheel was concealed within the body. Other models included V12 and V16.

32B Buick

32C Cadillac

THE New N.A. SERIES BUICK ARRIVES!
★ KNEE-ACTION WHEELS ★ NO-DRAUGHT VENTILATION
★ AUTOMATIC STARTING ★ STREAMLINE BEAUTY
★ EXHILARATING RESERVE OF POWER
80 M.P.H. SPEED — 20 M.P.H. COMFORT
COMFORT CATCHES UP WITH SPEED!
LENDRUM AND HARTMAN LTD.,
BUICK HOUSE, ALBEMARLE STREET, W.1
THE CAR THE WORLD RESPECTS
Buick
A RIDE IN THE NEW Buick IS A REVELATION

33A Buick

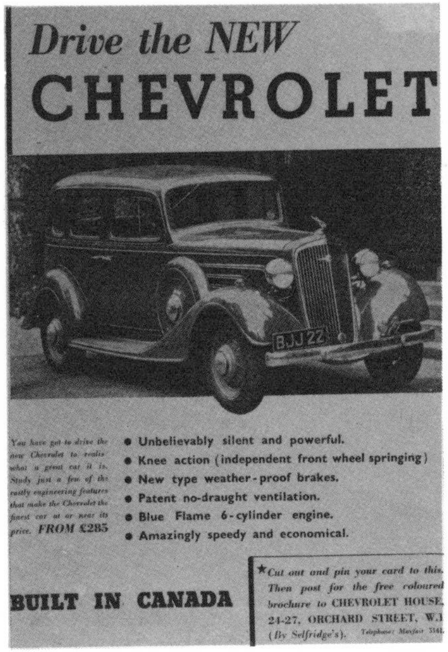
Drive the NEW
CHEVROLET
BJJ 22
You have got to drive the new Chevrolet to realise what a great car it is. Study just a few of the costly engineering features that make the Chevrolet the finest car at or near its price. FROM £285
● Unbelievably silent and powerful.
● Knee action (independent front wheel springing)
● New type weather-proof brakes.
● Patent no-draught ventilation.
● Blue Flame 6-cylinder engine.
● Amazingly speedy and economical.
BUILT IN CANADA
★Cut out and pin your card to this. Then post for the free coloured brochure to CHEVROLET HOUSE, 24-27, ORCHARD STREET, W.1 (By Selfridge's).

33B Chevrolet

33C Chevrolet

33D Chrysler

33A: **Buick,** built in Canada (McLaughlin, Series NA), was quite popular in Britain where several specimens still exist. Available were Series 50 (models 50, 56, 57, 58), Series 60 (models 61, 67) and Series 90 (models 90, 91), priced upwards from £505. They remained virtually unchanged for 1935.

33B: **Chevrolet Master Series DA** Sedan. Period advertisement of Canadian-built model for the British market. First Chevrolet with Dubonnet type independent front suspension. The Standard Series DC looked rather similar but was less luxurious and had a rigid front axle; mechanically it resembled the 1933 Standard.

33C: **Chevrolet Master Series DA** Town Sedan cost $635 and featured built-in trunk (boot) and wb 2 in. longer than 1933 model. 'Blue Flame' combustion chamber design raised power output to 80 bhp at 3300 rpm. Glove compartment could now be locked with a key. Weight 3130 lb.

33D: **Chrysler CA Six** Convertible Coupé with 3·95-litre engine. This particular car was originally supplied by the Chrysler dealer in Koblenz, Germany, and came to Britain in 1946. It was completely restored in 1965–66 and is shown here at the Pre-1950 American Auto Club's 1967 rally.

34A Chrysler

34B DeSoto

PH-AIP
34C DeSoto

34D Dodge

34A: **Chrysler Airflow CV Imperial** Sedan proved a costly 'white elephant' since it was way ahead of its time. There were also Eight (CU) and Custom Imperial (CX, CW) models.
34B: **DeSoto Airflow SE** Sedan. Other body style options: Coupé, two-door Brougham and Town Sedan. All models were powered by a 100-bhp six-cylinder L-head engine.
34C: **DeSoto Airflow SE** Town Sedan, with the famous Fokker F18 'Pelikaan' which flew from Amsterdam to Batavia (Dutch East Indies) delivering Christmas mail in 1933 in a record of four days 4½ hours.
34D: **Dodge DeLuxe DR Six** Sedan had new grille, front and rear vent windows and 117-in. wb. Engine output was 82 bhp. Also available 121-in. wb 87-bhp Six Special.

35A Ford

35B Ford

Alexis Kellner
Venlo

35C Ford

GFL 360D

35D Ford

**Ford Model 40** of 1934 resembled the 1933 model, except for the V8 badge on the radiator grille which was now a triangular shape (rather than 'cut-out'), the wheel hub covers and two hood handles at each side instead of one. It was also available with the four-cylinder engine. In Britain the 14·9 HP (Model 18) was continued alongside the Model 40.

35A: **Model 40 (Four)** with German bodywork by Papler. Four-cylinder models had oval Ford emblem on hub caps.

35B: **Model 40 (V8)** Sedan with sliding roof and large trunk was Dutch modification. Basically body style 730.

35C: **Model 40 (V8)** Convertible by Alexis Kellner, marketed on the Continent of Europe.

35D: **Model 40 (V8)** Roadster (710). Other Ford body styles included Coupés, Sedans (Tudor and Fordor), Victoria, Phaeton, Cabriolet.

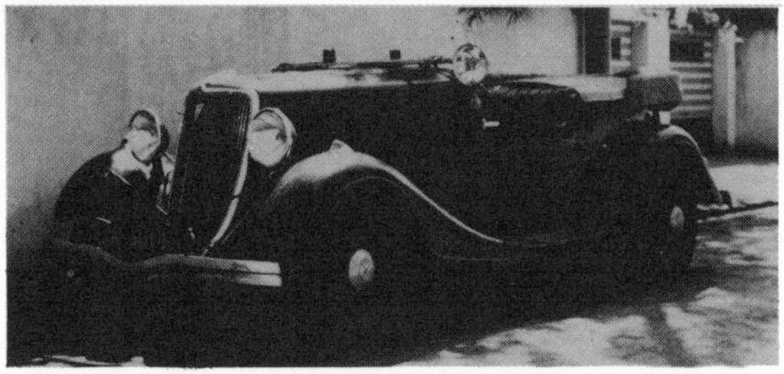
36A

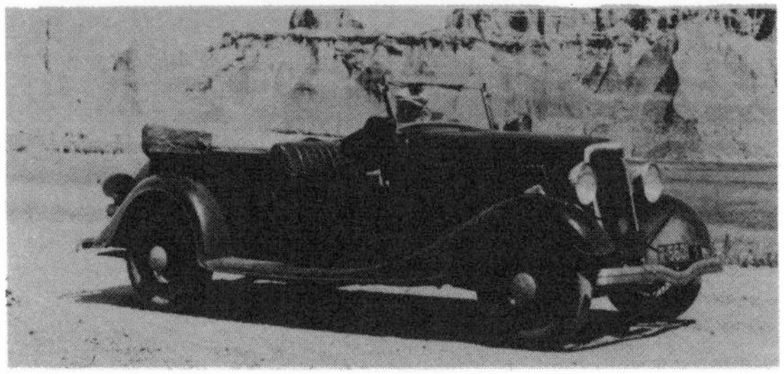
36B

36A, B, C: This 'one-off' **Ford Model 40 V8** Roadster was produced by the coach building firm of Schutter & van Bakel in Amsterdam to the design of its owner, the Dutch automotive engineer A. F. Loyens. The chassis was supplied by Ford's Amsterdam assembly plant. Mr Loyens used the car in various European countries and for a tour across the United States. Eventually he mounted the bodywork on a Hispano-Suiza chassis. Pictures show the car in France, USA (Rocky Mountains) and Switzerland. World-wide dealer network made the Ford an attractive car for such international use.

36C

36D Graham-Paige

36D: **Graham-Paige 'Blue Streak'** Six and Eight were in production from 1932–34, and pioneered the 'skirted fenders'. Many were exported.
36E: **Hudson Eight DeLuxe** Sedan had 108-bhp engine, 116-in. wb, and four forward-opening doors. Weight was 3020 lb, price $895.

36E Hudson

37A: **LaSalle Series 350D Eight** now had an in-line ('straight') engine and was also known as Series 50. It was produced by Cadillac on a 119-in. wb chassis with 'knee action' ifs.
37B: **Lincoln KB V12** Limousine shown in typical period advertisement. Two basic models were available, the 136-in. wb KA and the 145-in. wb KB, each with a variety of standard and custom-built bodies.

37C: **Nash Ambassador Eight** 1290 Sedan with Charles W. Nash (left) and E. H. McCarty, president of Nash Motors. Cheapest model was LaFayette.
37D: **Oldsmobile L34 Eight** Sedan had Fisher bodywork with re-styled front end. The 'All Feature Six' Model F34 was almost identical in appearance. The 'Knee Action' ifs is just visible.

37A LaSalle

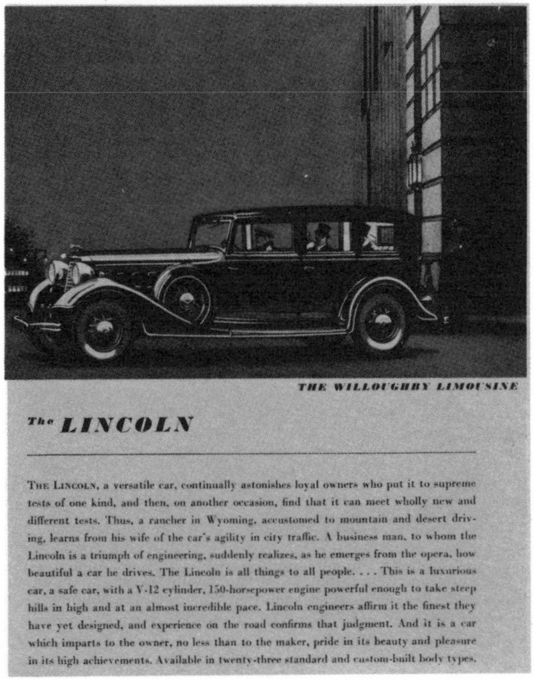
THE WILLOUGHBY LIMOUSINE
The LINCOLN
THE LINCOLN, a versatile car, continually astonishes loyal owners who put it to supreme tests of one kind, and then, on another occasion, find that it can meet wholly new and different tests. Thus, a rancher in Wyoming, accustomed to mountain and desert driving, learns from his wife of the car's agility in city traffic. A business man, to whom the Lincoln is a triumph of engineering, suddenly realizes, as he emerges from the opera, how beautiful a car he drives. The Lincoln is all things to all people. . . . This is a luxurious car, a safe car, with a V-12 cylinder, 150-horsepower engine powerful enough to take steep hills in high and at an almost incredible pace. Lincoln engineers affirm it the finest they have yet designed, and experience on the road confirms that judgment. And it is a car which imparts to the owner, no less than to the maker, pride in its beauty and pleasure in its high achievements. Available in twenty-three standard and custom-built body types.

37B Lincoln

37C Nash

37D Oldsmobile

G-306
Schutter & van Bakel

38A Packard

38A: **Packard Twelve, Eleventh Series** Touring Sedan by Schutter & van Bakel of Amsterdam, Netherlands. Note twin sliding-roof panels and built-in trunk. The V12 engine had a bore and stroke of $3\frac{7}{16} \times 4$ in. and developed 160 bhp at 3200 rpm. 11th Series production span: Aug. 1933–Aug. 1934.

38B: **Packard Eight, Eleventh Series** Sedan. There were several models, namely the 1100 (129-in. wb) Sedan, the 1101 (136-in. wb) with eleven body styles, the 1102 (141-in. wb) with two body styles, and the following Super Eight models: 1103 (135-in. wb) Sedan, 1104 (142-in. wb) with eleven body styles, 1105 Standard, Dietrich and LeBaron (all 147-in. wb) with ten body styles.

38B Packard

39A Studebaker

ALEXIS
KELLNER

39B Studebaker

39A: **Studebaker Commander Regal Eight** with Pennock bodywork, shown with top and side window guide rails folded down. Note all-metal cover on side-mounted spare wheel and V-shaped front bumper.
39B: **Studebaker Commander Regal Eight** Convertible with bodywork by Alexis Kellner exhibited in Dutch dealer's showroom. Body is strikingly similar to that of Pennock and other firms, including some in Great Britain.
39C: **Studebaker Commander Regal Eight** 119-in. wb chassis with Dutch Convertible bodywork by Pennock of The Hague. This type of bodywork was built on various American chassis by several European firms.
39D: **Terraplane Six** Convertible Coupé was entirely new and in styling looked much like its parent Hudson. Characteristic for 1934 model year was upright louvres in hood (bonnet) sides.

39C Studebaker

39D Terraplane

40A Auburn

Combined motor vehicle production during 1935 was not far below the four million mark. Total car, truck and bus registrations were the highest since 1930, at 26,227,000. Some three million autos now had radios and an AMA report disclosed that motorists now paid one of every eight tax dollars. 172,572 cars and chassis were exported. Technically there were few innovations but there was a trend toward two- and four-door Sedans and lower-priced less luxurious models with less powerful engines. Cadillac's medium-priced LaSalle, like most other GM products, now featured Fisher Bodies' 'Turret Top', which was an all-steel roof. Chrysler Corporation, smallest of the 'Big Three', exceeded its 1929 sales record for the third year in succession, although their total unit sales (Chrysler, DeSoto, Dodge and Plymouth) was well below that of Chevrolet and Ford. General Motors during 1935 recorded a total sales to dealers of 1,715,688 units, ranging from the cheapest Chevvy at $495 to the top-line Cadillac at $7750. Of this total, just over one million were Chevrolets. It was the Chevrolet Division's first million-plus year since 1929. Packard announced its low-price One Twenty car and saw annual production increase from 5,818 in 1934 to 52,256. Pontiac delivered its one millionth car (since 1926). The Ford Motor Company introduced its Lincoln Zephyr and participated in the 1935 National Automobile Show after having ignored national shows since early in the century. Nash offered a new type of 'seal-in' engine which meant that the conventional manifolding was cast inside the cylinder block.

---

AUBURN
with the
"6"
DUAL RATIO BACK AXLE
Vanity excused!
virtually – two cars in one
Vanity and car pride are a pardonable prerogative to the owner of the new Auburn Six. If you are honest and admit that you like a car for its appearance as well as its performance, then the ideal combination is now a practical possibility for around £380 instead of a dream in four figures.
The 1935 Auburn Six with the wonderful Dual-Ratio rear axle, which virtually gives you two cars in one, is beyond description. To merely recite its seventy-seven superlative features of mechanical design and its amazing combination of refinements is to waste words, while you might, and indeed should, be taking a trial run in one :—
.... which is the sole purpose of this advertisement. Give us a date and a time — anywhere to suit your convenience.
SINCLAIR MOTOR CONCESSIONS LTD.
OXFORD ROAD, CHISWICK, W.4 Telephone: CHISWICK 6010.
TAX: 6-Cyl. £23 (next year £17-5-0)
TAX: 8-Cyl. £30 (next year £22-10-0)
8-Cyl. models from £499.
(also with Dual Ratio)

40B Auburn

BYX 552

40C Buick

FK 6632

40D Buick

40A: **Auburn 851 Supercharged Speedster** was impressive 100-mph machine with a straight eight 150-bhp Lycoming engine. Fitted with supercharger and two-speed rear axle it was also available with other body styles.

40B: **Auburn** supplied six- and eight-cylinder models and they were also available in Britain as this period advertisement shows. Illustrated is the model 653 Sedan which cost £399. Wheelbase was 120 in.

40C: **Buick Eight NA Series** Convertible Coupé with rumble seat, model 56C, built in Canada for British market where it sold at £500. Price in the USA was $1230.

40D: **Buick Eight NA Series** Sedan. 1935 models were substantially the same as 1934. Most Buicks sold in Britain (with rhd) were produced in Canada and technically were McLaughlin-Buicks.

41A Chevrolet

41A: **Chevrolet Master Series EA** Coach with Dubonnet 'Knee Action' ifs and Fisher 'turret top' body. Master ED had rigid front axle.
41B: **Chevrolet Standard Series EC** resembled 1934 Standard DC and was continued as an economy model. Period advertisement lists Canadian products.
41C: **Chrysler Airstream** range was much more salable than contemporary Airflow models. In Britain they were known as 'Airglide Kingston'
41D: British **Chrysler Airflow** of 1935 was in fact 1934 DeSoto Airflow with 1935 model SG grille and 1934 Chrysler Airflow bumpers. They were assembled by Chrysler Motors Ltd in Kew, Surrey. The car shown is a rare survivor of this equally rare model.

41C Chrysler

CHEVROLET The Wonder Car
speed=boat acceleration . . . silence unbelievable
80 M-P-H 18 M-P-G £20 TAX
SALOONS FROM
£255
CHEVROLET
BUILT IN CANADA
Standard Model 2-seater £225
Standard Model 4-door Saloon £255
Master Model 4-door Saloon £285
Master Model 4-door Saloon de Luxe £310
COUPON
My present car is a Year
● Compare the Chevrolet feature by feature. Big, roomy all-steel Fisher body with patent no-draught ventilation ● Independent front-wheel springing on all Master models ● All-weather brakes and shock-proof steering ● Uncanny silence at all speeds ● Flashing acceleration like a speed-boat—smooth, tremendous ● You must experience the thrill of a Chevrolet. Trial runs any time, anywhere ● Write for fully-illustrated catalogue.
CHEVROLET HOUSE, 24-27, ORCHARD ST., W.1

41B Chevrolet

41D Chrysler

★ There's something in this
CHRYSLER
AIRFLOW
You've never known before—
★AUTOMATIC OVERDRIVE . . . AT OLYMPIA
STAND
117
Chrysler has done it again! Chrysler introduces the sensation of the 1934 Motor Show! Chrysler pioneers the Automatic Overdrive. Imagine a long, straight road ahead of you . . . . you accelerate . . . . the speedometer mounts to 45 miles an hour . . . and then, suddenly a miracle happens . . . your engine quietens . . . some invisible power is pulling you along with giant strides. Yet your engine seems almost idling as the speedometer soars, to 60-70-80 miles an hour! You have experienced the unforgettable thrill of Chrysler's new Overdrive Transmission. Entirely automatic, engaged by momentarily lifting your foot from the accelerator pedal at 45 m.p.h., it acts like an extra, ultra high gear. It saves engine wear, saves oil, saves petrol. It gives 60 miles an hour on second gear, over 90 miles an hour on top. An exclusive Chrysler feature, on Airflow models only. Even before the Show there has been a greater demand for the new Chrysler models than we ever expected. Come and see the whole Chrysler range at Olympia—prices from £277 up.
*Airflow models with Automatic Clutch and Free Wheeling but without Overdrive, are also available.*

42A Chrysler

42A: British **Chrysler Airflow** shown in this advertisement, which appeared at Motor Show time in October 1934, in fact shows what a 1934 DeSoto Airflow Coupé is. Components for British-assembled Chrysler products came from Canada but the end products differed from the American models in many details.

42B: **Chrysler Heston Airflow Eight** was the British designation for this 1934 Chrysler Airflow Eight. The advert appeared on the occasion of the Scottish Motor Show in November 1934. American Chrysler Airflow 1935 was face-lifted 1934 with Airstream-type grille.

42C: **DeSoto SF Airstream Six** had basically the same bodywork as the Chrysler Airstream. Body styles included Sedan (shown), Roadster and Coupé.

42D: **DeSoto SG Airflow Six** came in three models: Coupé, four-door Sedan (shown) and Town Sedan. Wheelbase was $115\frac{1}{2}$ in., piston displacement 241·5 cu in. (B×S $3\frac{3}{8} \times 4\frac{1}{2}$ in.) and power output 100 bhp at 3400 rpm. Front axle was rigid with leaf springs.

Have you seen the NEW "Overdrive"
CHRYSLER AIRFLOW?
ON STANDS
Nos 13, 20, 31
KELVIN HALL
GLASGOW
TOGETHER WITH A WONDERFUL RANGE OF OTHER
CHRYSLER CARS
These are the cars with an automatic overdrive that gives a real 60 m.p.h. on second, and in some models over 90 m.p.h. on top. So comfortable you can read a paper at 80 m.p.h. in the back seat!
Then there are the famous Kew Sixes—now greater value than ever—the lowest priced Six in Chrysler history—the Richmond and Kingston Sixes, most beautiful cars of conventional design that Chrysler has ever produced. Prices range from £277.
The "Heston" Airflow Eight £625.
CHRYSLER

42B Chrysler

42C DeSoto

42D DeSoto

43A Dodge

"SPEED"-SILENCE-COMFORT THAT WILL AMAZE YOU
"Synchromatic Control"
EXCLUSIVE TO THE
DODGE
"Jubilee Six"
Improved gearbox and gear change, ultra-light clutch, cross-type steering and powerful toe-action hydraulic brakes—these factors combine to create the amazing "Synchromatic Control" on the latest Dodge. You've never really driven a car until you have tried it. This feature, with the novel stabilized suspension system and superb engine performance, alone would make this car outstanding. But add a host of luxury comfort refinements and a beautiful streamlined appearance, and you'll have some idea of why we're so pleased with the "Jubilee Six." Call in and see for yourself.
The "Jubilee Six" has these important new features :—
★ Synchromatic Control.
★ Tubular front axle and stabilized suspension
★ 25.3 H.P. or 19.8 H.P. engine to choice.
★ 12-volt electrical equipment.
★ Filtered air ventilation system.
PRICES FROM £330.
AN EXPERIENCE THAT AWAITS YOU AT
Jack Olding & CO. LTD
Sole Concessionnaires for London and the Home Counties.
75/6, HIGH STREET, MARYLEBONE, LONDON, W.1.
Telephone : Welbeck 5441/2/3.

43B Dodge

43C Ford

43D Ford

43A: **Dodge DU Six** was only 1935 Dodge model, with choice of various body styles. Engine was 3569-cc L-head (export option: DV 2794-cc).
43B: British **Dodge 'Jubilee Six'** series comprised 25·3 HP Senior Six (3569-cc) and 19·8 HP Victory Six (small-bore 2794-cc).
43C: **Ford Model 48** (V8, 3·6-litre, 30HP) and British **Model 60** (V8, 2·2-litre, 22HP) looked identical. Wheelbase was 112 in.
43D: **Ford V8** Special coachbuilt seven-seater limousine was offered 'finished to your choice' by W. Harold Perry Ltd of London N. 12.
43E: **Graham** offered various six- and eight-cylinder models but during 1935 the Eight was replaced by a supercharged Six.

THE NEW 21·6 H.P.
GRAHAM
21·6 H.P. De Luxe Saloon from £316
OTHER MODELS & PRICES
26 H.P. Special Six Saloon „ £395
26 H.P. Special Six Coupe „ £425
34 H.P. Supercharged Saloon „ £535
34 H.P. Supercharged Convertible Coupe „ £565
A GRAHAM-PAIGE QUALITY PRODUCTION PROVIDING A MAGNIFICENT PERFORMANCE WITH A MODEST TAX AND LOW FUEL CONSUMPTION.
A worthy companion to the famous Supercharged Eight and Special Six, this junior model within a few weeks of its introduction in South Africa was the only car to complete the strenuous Capetown-Johannesburg-Capetown Trial without loss of a single point, averaging 23 m.p.g. over 2,000 miles running.
All Graham models are low built and wide tracked to hold the road with comfort and safety—Graham engines are vibrationless at speed and supremely smooth at low speeds under heavy load. The Supercharger is silent and trouble free, promotes economy at speed and commands the road.
Sole Concessionnaires Great Britain and Northern Ireland.
CLEVERLYS LTD.
32, St. Mary Abbot's Terrace, W.14.
300 yards East of OLYMPIA Main Road Entrance

43E Graham

AN
EXCEPTIONALLY
WIDE RANGE
OF MODELS
Hudson built cars have attracted world wide admiration for their uncanny silence and brilliant performance. Further distinctiveness is given to Terraplane and Hudson cars by the wide range of models and coachwork that is available, enabling the buyer to choose the model that exactly meets his requirements. A few popular designs are here illustrated.
FOUR DOOR SALOON
Terraplanes from £299
Hudsons „ £360
FIXED HEAD COUPE
(with dickey)
Hudson 8 £395
CONVERTIBLE COUPE
(with dickey)
Terraplane £345
Hudson 8 £410
SPECIAL OPEN SPORTS
Terraplane £375
DROP-HEAD FOURSOME
Terraplane £425
Hudson 8 £495
For particulars of other styles write to:—
HUDSON MOTORS LIMITED
Great West Road, London, W.4 (Chiswick 4777)
West End Showrooms: Shaw & Kilburn Ltd.
117 Great Portland Street, W.1
TERRAPLANE & HUDSON

44A Hudson

44A: **Hudson** and **Terraplane** came in a wide variety of models including a Panel Delivery Van. Period advertisement shows some of the models offered on the British market including British special open sports and drophead bodywork on certain chassis (see also page 47).
44B: **Hudson Six** Sedan. In 1935 Hudson introduced the 'Electric Hand' finger-tip control for gear shifting. Year's sales included 101,080 cars and 1281 commercial vehicles. The company reported that it now had 3225 Hudson-Terraplane dealers in the United States.
44C: **Hudson Eight DeLuxe Brougham** was top-line model which in Britain was offered at £499, including radio, in December 1934. 'Glide uphill at eighty miles an hour or more without a trace of mechanical noise to mar your enjoyment'.

44B Hudson

44C Hudson

ANNOUNCING
THE NEW 4-LITRE
£375
THE CAR OF THE LINE
AERODYNAMIC
HUPMOBILE
THE MOST BEAUTIFUL OF THE AIR MINDED CARS
To this new Hupmobile belongs a new interpretation of motoring .... No longer are you conscious of a toiling mechanism—of laboured motion. Rather is it the road itself that streaks away behind you. Yet if the spirit of this car is of the sky .... its lines are sanely down to earth—air-moulded without freakishness or exaggeration.
You are cordially invited to examine this notable car—to put it through its paces on the road before deciding on any other car.
PRICES
Series 527 T, 8-cyl. 6-seater 4-door Saloon £595, 8-cyl. Coupe £595. Series 521 J, Saloon £475, Coupe £505
New 4-Litre 6-seater Saloon £375. De Luxe Models £398. Long Wheelbase 7-passenger Limousine £895
SOLE CONCESSIONAIRES INTERNATIONAL DISTRIBUTORS LTD., 43 BERKELEY STREET, LONDON W.1.
45A Hupmobile

45A: **Hupmobile** introduced new departure in aerodynamic styling. Headlamp/hood styling was later copied by Opel and Renault. British advertisement.
45B: **International C-1** was a commercial chassis which was sometimes used for special bodywork such as taxicab and military scout car (shown).
45C: **LaFayette Six** was low-price line of Nash, 1934–39. In 1935 there were eight body styles, all on 113-in. wb chassis.
45D: **LaSalle Series 50 Eight** did not differ much from 1934 model year, the main exterior difference being styling of bumpers.
45E: **Lincoln KB V12 Touring** was seven-passenger 'Royalty Special' on 145-wb chassis. Peculiar side windows retracted in the doors.
45F: **Nash** in 1935 had 'Aeroform' styling and offered only two- and four-door Sedans (Advanced Six and Eight and Ambassador Eight).

45D LaSalle

45E Lincoln

45B International

45C LaFayette

45F Nash

46A: **Oldsmobile F35 Six and L35 Eight** featured Fisher 'Turret Top' all-steel roof, in common with most other GM cars from the 1935 model year.
46B: **Packard One Twenty (120A), Twelfth Series** Touring Sedan, body style 892. Six alternative body types. 8-in-line engine, developing 110 bhp. Wheelbase 120 in.
46C: **Packard Eight 1201, Twelfth Series** Convertible Victoria, body style 807. Wheelbase 134 in. (Model 1200: 127 in., Model 1202: 139 in.). Also Super Eight and Twelve ranges of models.
46D: **Packard One Twenty** was Packard's entry into the low-price field. Prices started at $980 (Business Coupé). Just under 25,000 produced, many for export.

46A Oldsmobile

46B Packard

BXN 99

46C Packard

TO-DAY'S MOST WIDELY DISCUSSED CAR
The Packard "120," the world's newest motor car! It has been planned to fit the 1935 requirements of those who want a finer car than has yet been available in the lower priced field.
The Packard "120" is a worthy member of a distinguished family. It bears the finest name in motoring. Modern and luxurious in appearance, it delivers outstanding performance, safety, ease of riding and driving, and economy of operation. It is Packard-designed and Packard-built—not an assembled car.
Complete specifications and prices will be available shortly. May we post you this information?
PACKARD-"120"
SOLE CONCESSIONAIRES
LEONARD WILLIAMS & CO. LTD.
Head Office: Great West Road, Brentford, Middlesex
Scottish Depot: Corstorphine Road, Murrayfield, Edinburgh
London Showrooms: Berkeley Street, W.1

46D Packard

47A: **Plymouth PJ Six DeLuxe Voyager** Sedan was one of Chrysler's best selling models. Marketed in Britain as Chrysler Kew Six and Wimbledon Six.
47B: **Pontiac 701 Six** Sedan was one of seven body styles available in 1935. Eight-cylinder versions (Series 605) were also available. Bodies by Fisher, Dubonnet-type ifs.
47C: **Studebaker Commander Eight** Sedan. Car shown has non-original headlamps. Other 1935 'Studes' included Dictator and President with various body styles topped by Land Cruiser Sedans.
47D: **Terraplane Six** was popular in Hudson's home and export markets, including Britain where this Sedan sold at around £300. Engine was 2597-cc 16·9 HP or 3455-cc 21·6 HP (Big Six).
47E: **Terraplane Six** Panel Delivery was basically passenger car with modified rear body. Hudson Motor Co. produced light commercial vehicles from 1929 (Dover) until 1947.

47A Plymouth

ABB·18·14
47C Studebaker

OW 6830
47D Terraplane

47B Pontiac

47E Terraplane

# 1936

Sales this year increased again, final production figures showing 3,669,528 cars (about 95% of which were priced below $750 wholesale) and 784,587 trucks and buses. Wholesale value of replacement parts and accessories also rose again, by 21·5%. Exports of cars and chassis totalled 179,957 units. Buick produced its three millionth car and offered flashing direction indicators (turn signals) incorporated in the transparent red plastic 'wings' of the Buick emblem on the trunk (boot) lid. Chevrolet produced over 1¼ million cars and trucks, including the firm's 12 millionth vehicle. This GM division led the industry in sales for the eighth time in 10 years and their dealer profits reached a new all-time high. The Chrysler Corporation sold more than one million vehicles for the first time in its history. Hudson patented its 'Triple-Safe' brake system and produced 123,266 cars. Most of these were Terraplanes (93,309) which came in 27 models starting with a Business Coupé at $695. It was Hudson's peak year of the decade. Nash, of Kenosha, merged with the Kelvinator Corp. of Detroit and became the Nash-Kelvinator Corp. Packard introduced its Six '110', the lowest priced Packard ever offered, and saw sales jump to over 80,000 units. For Studebaker 1936 marked the sharpest increase in business in the firm's history: car sales went up by 71·5%, trucks by 26·5%. Willys-Overland was re-organised and as Willys-Overland Motors Inc. introduced its new little 'Surprise Car of the Year', the Model 77, at the New York Auto Show in November.

---

48A: **Auburn** Phaeton as produced during 1935 and 1936. Car shown was experimentally fitted with a diesel engine by the Cummins Engine Company in 1935, replacing the original 'Straight 8'.
48B: **Buick Eight** with custom-built Convertible bodywork by Schutter & van Bakel of Amsterdam. American GM cars for the Benelux countries were (and are) mostly assembled by General Motors Continental S.A. in Antwerp.
48C: **Buick Eight Series 90 Limited** Eight-passenger Sedan with built-in trunk (Model 90) was one of Buick's top-line models. A six-seater (91) and a Limousine (90L) were also available.

CUMMINS DIESEL
First DIESEL POWERED
PASSENGER CAR
48A Auburn

48B Buick

48C Buick

49A: **Buick Eight Series 90** Limousine as used by the Duke of Windsor (then King Edward VIII). Like the Series 60 Century and 80 Roadmaster it had an in-line ohv engine rated at 37·8 HP.
49B: Interior of the **Buick 90** Limousine provided a high degree of privacy. Once the Duke of Windsor's private car, it was auctioned in 1969 and commanded a price of £2,300.

49C: **Cadillac V8** came in three Series: 60 (shown), 70 and 75 with wb lengths of 121, 131 and 138 in. respectively. Series 80 and 85 were V12, Series 90 was V16.
49D: **Cadillac** Limousine used by the late Princess (then Queen) Wilhelmina of the Netherlands had various modifications. In the USA this year 48·1% of all cars sold above $1500 were Cadillacs.

49A Buick

49C Cadillac

49B Buick

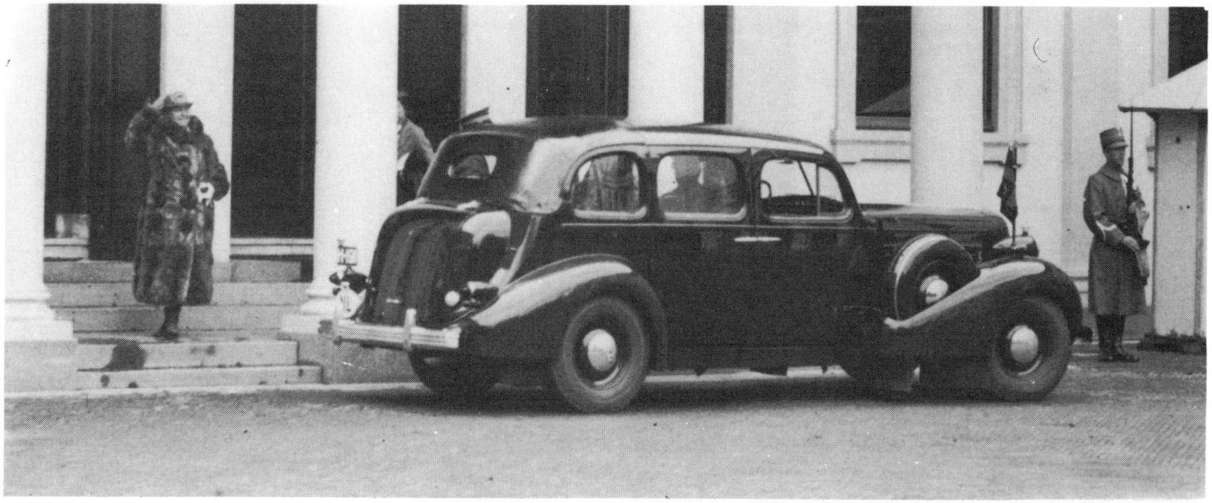
49D Cadillac

## 1936

50A: **Chevrolet Master** had Dubonnet ifs (Series FA) or rigid front axle (FD). Cheaper FC Standard Series had similar bodywork but 109– (vs 113–) in. wb and 5·25 (vs 5·50)×17 tyres.
50B: **Chevrolet Master Imperial** was GM Continental's lwb (124 in.) model, shod with 6·00×17 tyres. Shown is the Cabriolet.
50C: **Chevrolet Standard FC** Cabriolet (one of seven FC body options) shared 206-cu in. 'Stove Bolt Six' with FA and FD Series.
50D: British **Chrysler Wimbledon Six Airglide** was basically a Plymouth. Other 1935 British Chryslers: Kew, Richmond and Croydon (all Sixes), Heston Airflow 8 and Royal Airflow. Prices £289–£725.

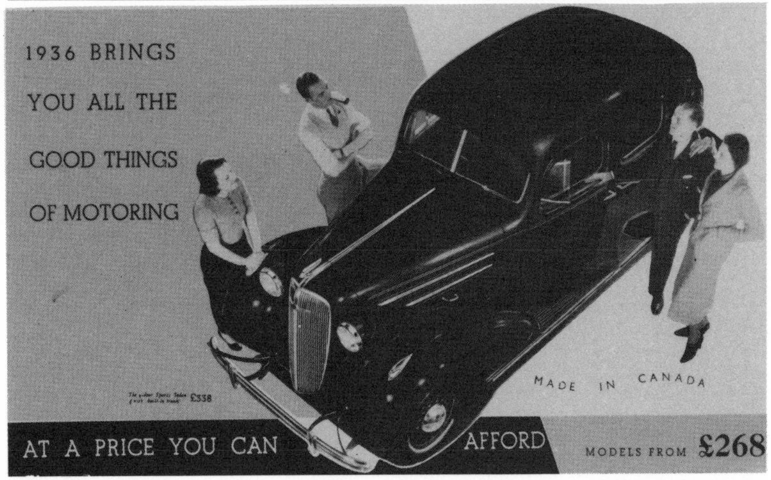
1936 BRINGS
YOU ALL THE
GOOD THINGS
OF MOTORING
MADE IN CANADA
AT A PRICE YOU CAN
AFFORD
MODELS FROM £268
50A Chevrolet

50B Chevrolet

DUM 231
50C Chevrolet

CLK 593
50D Chrysler

51A: **Chrysler C8 Airstream DeLuxe Eight** Traveller Sedan was one of a wide range of 'conventional' models. Six-cylinder models (C7) had different hub caps and hood louvres. 'Airwheel' 6·50 × 16 tyres.
51B: **Chrysler C9 Airflow Eight** Sedan. Other 1936 Chrysler Airflows were the C10 Imperial and C11 Custom Imperial. Model shown had $122\frac{13}{16}$-in. wb and 323·5-cu in. in-line engine developing 115 bhp at 3400 rpm.

51C: **DeSoto S1 Custom Airstream Six** Sedan. Also available was a DeLuxe Airstream which had single-piece windshield. Technically the DeSoto, Dodge and Plymouth (all Chrysler products) had much in common.
51D: **DeSoto S2 Airflow** Sedan was also available in two-door form, termed Coupé. 5000 S2 cars were built in this, the last year of the DeSoto Airflows.

CHRYSLER
DeLuxe 8
TRAVELER SEDAN
51A Chrysler

51B Chrysler

51C DeSoto

51D DeSoto

52A: **Dodge D2 Six** Sedan was available in Great Britain as a Saloon or as a Limousine with division. A small-bore export engine (23·4 HP) was also available, designated Model D3.
52B: **Dodge D2 Six** Sedan had 217·8 cu-in. (25·3 HP) L-head engine, developing 87 bhp at 3600 rpm. In Britain it was known as the Senior Six.
52C: **Fargo FD1-16** was attractive looking Parcel Van based on Chrysler Plymouth car chassis. Chrysler used Fargo name for certain commercial, export and military vehicles.
52D: **Ford Model 68 V8** had 112-in. wb and the catalogue listed 16 body styles including this Type 760 Cabriolet. They all had the 3·6-litre (30HP) engine.
52E: **Ford Model 68 V8** Fordor Sedan, Type 730. There were Standard and DeLuxe versions of the Tudor (700) and Fordor Sedans and Touring Sedans.
53A: **Graham Series 110 Supercharger Six** models were introduced in 1935, replacing the former Eight models. Eight, however, was still available in Britain by mid-1936.
53B: **International C-1** with taxicab bodywork for use in Norway. 'Airwheels' had 7·00 × 15 tyres. Basically this was a 125-in. wb light truck chassis.
53C: **LaFayette Six 3618** was four-door Sedan made by Nash on 113-in. wb and billed as 'the big car in the low price field'.

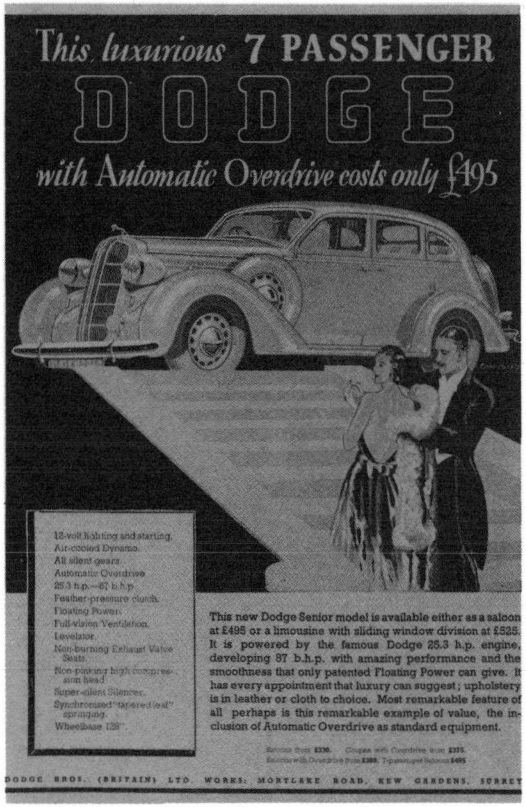
This luxurious 7 PASSENGER
DODGE
with Automatic Overdrive costs only £495
12-volt lighting and starting.
Air-cooled Dynamo.
All silent gears
Automatic Overdrive
25.3 h.p.—87 b.h.p.
Feather-pressure clutch.
Floating Power.
Full-vision Ventilation.
Levelator.
Non-burning Exhaust Valve Seats.
Non-pinking high compression head
Super-silent Silencer.
Synchronised "tapered leaf" springing.
Wheelbase 128".
This new Dodge Senior model is available either as a saloon at £495 or a limousine with sliding window division at £525. It is powered by the famous Dodge 25.3 h.p. engine, developing 87 b.h.p. with amazing performance and the smoothness that only patented Floating Power can give. It has every appointment that luxury can suggest; upholstery is in leather or cloth to choice. Most remarkable feature of all perhaps is this remarkable example of value, the inclusion of Automatic Overdrive as standard equipment.
DODGE BROS. (BRITAIN) LTD. WORKS: MORTLAKE ROAD, KEW GARDENS, SURREY
52A Dodge

52B Dodge

52C Fargo

CYH 303
52D Ford

52E Ford

53D: **LaSalle Series 50 Eight** Coupé with 120-in. wb. This was the last year in which Cadillac produced an in-line Eight. Typical list price $1225.
53E: **Lincoln Zephyr Model H V12** was first introduced by the Ford Motor Co. for the 1936 model year. This ultra-streamlined 122-in. wb Sedan was 202½ in. long.

53F: **Lincoln KA** Phaeton featured 67° V12 engine with $3\frac{1}{8} \times 4\frac{1}{2}$ in. bore and stroke giving a piston displacement of 414 cu in. Compression ratio was 5·25:1, output 150 bhp at 3400 rpm.
53G: **Nash DeLuxe 400 Six** two-door Sedan model 3645A had 117-in. wb. Ambassador Six and Super Eight had 125-in. wb. Total Nash sales: 53,038.

Experience Silent Supercharged Performance with Economy on the
Graham 26 h.p. Super Six
The Graham Supercharger is a simple piece of mechanism proved over 2½ years and 50 million miles. It is a perfect mixer and a petrol saver, evening out the normal irregularities of carburation and eliminating waste; 26 m.p.g. and more has been registered in official tests.
PRICES
26 h.p. Super Six Saloon £445
26 h.p. Six Saloon £395
22 h.p. Six Saloon £328
Overdrive on 26 h.p. models £15 extra.
34 h.p. G.B.S. Eight (GRAHAM BRITISH SPECIAL) Chassis £485 Saloon £750
Sole Concessionaires for Great Britain and
CLEVERLYS LTD.
32, ST. MARY ABBOT'S TERRACE, W.14
300 yards East of Olympia Main Road Entrance

53A Graham

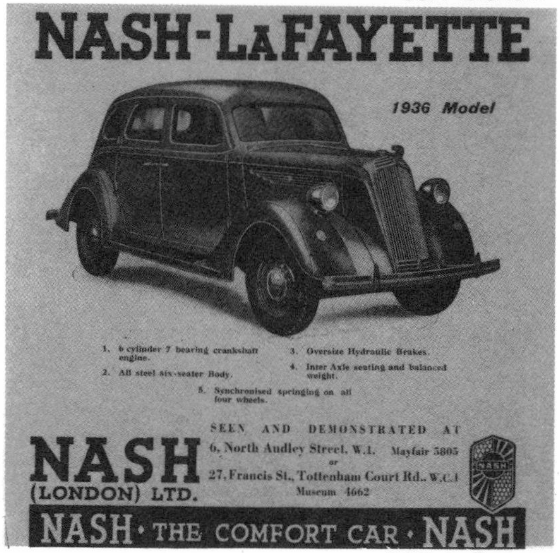
NASH-LAFAYETTE
1936 Model
1. 6 cylinder 7 bearing crankshaft engine.
2. All steel six-seater Body.
3. Oversize Hydraulic Brakes.
4. Inter Axle seating and balanced weight.
5. Synchronised springing on all four wheels.
SEEN AND DEMONSTRATED AT
6, North Audley Street, W.1. Mayfair 5805
or
27, Francis St., Tottenham Court Rd., W.C.1
Museum 4662
NASH (LONDON) LTD.
NASH · THE COMFORT CAR · NASH

53C LaFayette

53B International

53F Lincoln

53D LaSalle

53E Lincoln

53G Nash

54A: **Oldsmobile F36 Six and L36 Eight** had open coil spring ifs and wb sizes of 115 and 121 in. respectively. A wide range of all-steel Fisher bodies was available.
54B: **Packard Super Eight, Fourteenth Series** was in production from August 1935 until September 1936. There were three models, 1403 (132-in. wb), 1404 (139-in. wb) and 1405 (144-in. wb) with 17 body styles.
54C: **Pierce-Arrow 1601 Eight** Club Sedan with 144-in. wb chassis had 150-bhp engine plus power brakes with vacuum booster and a host of other safety features and luxury fittings. 1602 and 1603 were V12s.
54D: **Plymouth P1 Six** Station Wagon could carry seven to eight passengers. Also available on the same 113-in. wb chassis was a steel-panelled Commercial Sedan (also known as Sedan Delivery).

F 2412
54A Oldsmobile

54B Packard

54C Pierce-Arrow

54D Plymouth

55A: **Pontiac Master and DeLuxe Six and Eight** had Dubonnet type ifs, L-head (side-valve) engines of 27·4 and 33·8 HP rating and 'Silver Streak' bodywork by Fisher.
55B: **Pontiac Eight Silver Streak** two-door Sedan, was one of seven body styles available on the Eight with 116$\frac{5}{8}$-in. wb and also on the Six (Master and DeLuxe) with 112-in. wb.

55C: **Terraplane Six** was shaped like the contemporary Hudson but lower in price. Wheelbase was 115 in. and engine output 88 bhp with an optional 100. Two-door Sedan version was termed Brougham.
55D: **Terraplane Six** Station Wagon helped Hudson Motor Co. to increase sales to almost 25% above the previous year. All doors were forward-opening. Wheels were 'easy-clean' type.

55A Pontiac

55B Pontiac

55C Terraplane

55D Terraplane

## 1937

1937 saw another increase in US motor vehicle sales: 3,915,889 cars, and 893,085 trucks and buses. Ford could claim highest total sales (although Chevrolet sold more cars, Ford sold more trucks, just enough to beat Chevrolet's overall figure). The battle for leadership between Ford and Chevrolet was always fierce. It is interesting to compare these two cars, technically. In 1937 their share of overall US car sales was: Chevrolet 22·05%, Ford 21·99%. Yet, compared with the present time, these two cars were different in so many respects that millions of people had developed a kind of loyalty towards either one or the other. Ford introduced a V8 engine in 1932 whereas Chevrolet had built Sixes ever since 1929 and did not offer an optional V8 until 1955 (except for a few in 1917–19). Fords had alligator-type hoods (bonnets) and built-in headlamps from 1937, Chevrolet not until 1940–41. Fords had a manual starter from 1937, Chevrolet stuck to a pedal until 1949. Other characteristic Ford features were their split-type rear axle, side valves, round pedal pads, steering column-mounted ignition switch (1932–48) and transversal road springs with 'live' front axle (1906–48). Chevrolets had longitudinal leaf springs with ifs on top-line models from 1934 (all from 1941), banjo-type rear axles, overhead valves and oblong pedal pads. Number three US car, Chrysler's Plymouth (13·27% of 1937 total sales) was different again and some of its distinguishing features were a side-valve Six engine with high-up starter pedal, parking brake behind the gearbox, open prop shaft and semi-elliptics all round (until 1939). Each of these three marques had its own individual 'personality' with distinguishing engine sound, handling and 'feel'.

56A Buick

56A: **Buick Eight Series 60 Century** Touring Sedan model 61 with trunk and fender well. In the USA this 3975-lb car cost $1105 Six other body styles, including Convertible Phaeton.

56B: Canadian **Buick (McLaughlin) Series CO** with British Albemarle Drop Head Coupé bodywork. 1937 Buick series and wb lengths: 40 Special (122 in.), 60 Century (126 in.), 80 Roadmaster (131 in.), 90 Limited (138 in.).

56C: **Cadillac V8** came in four series and wb lengths, namely 60 (124 in.), 65 (131 in.), 70 (131 in.) and 75 (138 in.). In addition there were the 85 (V12, 138 in.) and 90 (V16, 154 in.), and LaSalle 50 (V8, 124 in.). Shown: Series 70.

EGT 113

56B Buick

DT 8898

56C Cadillac

57A: **Chevrolet 'Cheetah'** was Canadian export model with 81 instead of 88·9 mm cylinder bore, resulting in 24·4 instead of 29·3 HP treasury rating. It was available in the UK only during 1937 and part of 1938.

57B: **Chevrolet Master DeLuxe Series GA** with custom-built coachwork by van Rijswijk in the Netherlands. Series GA had Dubonnet ifs; Master Series GB had rigid front axle, otherwise basically similar.

57C: **Cord 812,** shown with some later modifications, was powered by Lycoming L-head V8 engine, driving the front wheels. Headlamps were retractable. Also available with closed bodywork. First introduced in 1935 (810).

57D: **Cord 812 Phaeton** side view showing alligator-type hood and exposed exhaust pipes. The 4730-cc standard engine produced 125 bhp but with optional supercharger power was up to 195 bhp.

Announcing the new, brilliant
CHEVROLET
the 24 h.p. 'CHEETAH'
New economy now added to Chevrolet
spaciousness and speed
Year by year, Chevrolet have broken all records for luxuriousness and good value. But now comes the "Cheetah", with all Chevrolet distinguishing features and the new economy of a 24 h.p. engine.
The "Cheetah" has been specially produced to meet the needs of the British motorist—it is economical but with all the swift, graceful performance that the name implies. Sleek and tuned to a hair's breadth, it is away into swift silent movement in a flash. Smooth and sure-footed over the roughest surfaces, it will stop dead, at need, in its tracks. With this splendid performance and new added economy, the Chevrolet "Cheetah" is more than ever the logical choice of the discerning motorist.
£318
SOLE CONCESSIONAIRES FOR THE UNITED KINGDOM
PASS AND JOYCE
CHEVROLET HOUSE, 24-27 ORCHARD STREET, W.1
SEE THE NEW 'CHEETAH' AT STAND 78, MOTOR SHOW, EARLS COURT
57A Chevrolet

57B Chevrolet

QUEBEC 40
55-751
57C Cord

57D Cord

## 1937

58A: **Chrysler Imperial Eight** was top-line model. Car shown was seen in Spain, powered by a Barreiros diesel engine. This year also saw the last Airflow cars, the Chrysler C17. Total Airflow output from 1934 was 29,928 Chryslers, 25,737 DeSotos.
58B: **DeSoto S3 DeLuxe Six** had 3·74-litre 93-bhp power unit and 116-in. wb (except Seven-Place Sedan shown, which had 133-in. wb and glass partition). Other body styles included two- and four-door Sedans, Convertible Sedan and various Coupés.
58C: **DeSoto SP Six** was special export model with four body styles (Sedan, Touring Sedan, Two-door Sedan, Coupé with Dickey-Seat) and was in effect a slightly modified Plymouth. It had a 3·3-litre 78-bhp L-head engine and wb was 112 in.
58D: **Dodge D5 DeLuxe Six** had 3·6-litre engine and 116- or 133-in. wb. Available for export was a 112-in. wb model (Dodge D6 Six or Victory) which had a smaller-bore 3·3 litre engine. Like the DeSoto SP this smaller Dodge was basically a Plymouth.

58A Chrysler

58B DeSoto

58C DeSoto

58D Dodge

59A Ford

ELF 316
819 HO

59B Ford

59C Ford

59D Graham

59E Hudson

59A: **Ford V8 Model 78** and **Model 74** were identical in appearance except for badge on radiator grille which showed engine type (60 or 85 bhp). British Model 74 (30 HP) shown.
59B: **Ford V8 Model 78** Station Wagon as produced by Ford of Britain. Offically termed Utility, these models were popularly known as 'Woodies'. Note modified headlamps.
59C: **Ford V8 Model 78** Station Wagon, body type 790. This model was built in Britain and fitted with special 9·00 × 13 tyres for use by the British Army.
59D: **Graham Super Custom Six** had super-charged engine of 3560 cc cubic capacity. Maximum output was 116 bhp at 4000 rpm. Unusual body design was by Amos Northup.
59E: **Hudson Eight** Convertible Brougham. Optional equipment included the 'Electric Hand' automatic gear shift. Hudson Eights were available with two wb lengths, 122 and 129 in.
59F: **LaSalle Series 50 V8** Coupé. After three years of straight eights, the LaSalle was powered by a V8 engine again. Wheelbase was 124 in., typical list price $1260.

59F LaSalle

60A: **Lincoln Zephyr HB V12** Two-door Sedan, fitted with sunroof (Dutch modification). As can be seen, the European Ford V8 models (page 75) had several styling features in common with the Zephyr.
60B: **Lincoln Zephyr HB V12** Coupé had exceptionally long 'rear deck'. Note also the streamlined rear light units and the rear wheel cover panels which came as standard equipment.
60C: **Lincoln Zephyr HB V12** Sedan had 122-in. wb, 133-in. springbase (road springs were transversal, as on Ford). Overall length was 210 in, width 73 in., and the Sedan weighed about 3490 lb.

60D: **Oldsmobile F37 Six and L37 Eight** shared Fisher bodyshells with contemporary Buicks. These were different from those used by Chevrolet and Pontiac. Olds Six and Eight wb was 117 and 124 in. respectively.

60A Lincoln

EXB 65

60B Lincoln

HV 8808

60C Lincoln

60D Oldsmobile

61A: **Packard Eight (One Twenty), Fifteenth Series, Model 120C** Convertible Coupé. Wheelbase 120 in. Nine body styles.
61B: **Packard Super Eight, Fifteenth Series, Model 1501** Club Sedan. Wheelbase 134 in. Engine: 135 bhp at 3200 rpm.
61C: **Packard Super Eight, Fifteenth Series, Model 1500** Touring Sedan. Wheelbase 127 in. Model 1502 had 139-in. wb.
61D: **Packard Six (One Ten), Fifteenth Series, Model 115C (110)** Four-door Sedan was one of eight body styles available on this 115-in. wb chassis. L-head engine developed 100 bhp.
61E: **Plymouth Six** Photo shows Mr Piet Olyslager as free-lance motoring journalist with DeLuxe Sedan on Mont Ventoux, France. In Britain this model was named Chrysler Kew Six.

DYE 21
61A Packard

BAC 963
61B Packard

61C Packard

61D Packard

L-29158
61E Plymouth

## 1937

62A: **Pontiac Silver Streak** was again available as either a Six (wb 117 in.) or Eight (wb 122 in.). There were eight common body styles. Station Wagon came only as Six.
62B: **Pontiac Silver Streak** was also available in Britain, with right-hand drive. Silver Streak name indicated Pontiac's characteristic band of chrome mouldings over grille and hood.
62C: **Studebaker Six and Eight** were offered in Great Britain, starting from £458. The model shown in this advertisement of July 1937 shows convertible coachwork by Salmons.
62D: **Studebaker President Eight** had 4·1-litre engine and 125- or 143-in. wb. Dictator Six models had 3·6-litre engine, 116-in. wb. Windshield washers were offered for the first time.

62A Pontiac

PONTIAC
Silver Streak
GENERAL MOTORS' MASTERPIECE
THE MOST BEAUTIFUL
THING ON WHEELS
Saloons from £365 • Coupés from £355
U.S. CONCESSIONAIRES LTD.
36, Berkeley Street, London, W.1.
Telephone: Mayfair 5906-7.
Service Depot: Jubilee Place, Chelsea, S.W.3.
Telephone: Flaxman 7380.
London Distributors:
THE MOTOR COMBINE, 365, EUSTON RD., N.W.1.
Telephone: Euston 4141.
Scottish and Border Counties Distributors:
ROSSLEIGH LTD., 32, Shandwick Place, Edinburgh.
OLYMPIA
STAND
103

62B Pontiac

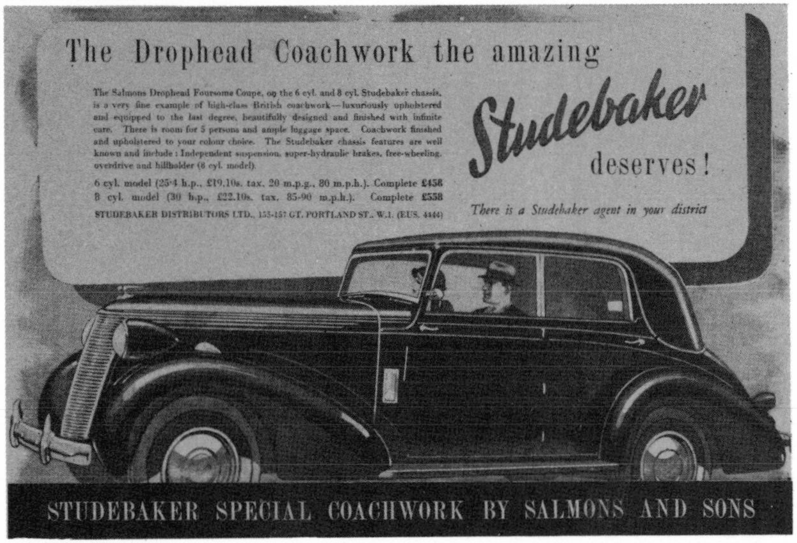
The Dropheaad Coachwork the amazing
Studebaker
deserves!
The Salmons Dropheaad Foursome Coupe, on the 6 cyl. and 8 cyl. Studebaker chassis, is a very fine example of high-class British coachwork—luxuriously upholstered and equipped to the last degree, beautifully designed and finished with infinite care. There is room for 5 persons and ample luggage space. Coachwork finished and upholstered to your colour choice. The Studebaker chassis features are well known and include: Independent suspension, super-hydraulic brakes, free-wheeling, overdrive and hillholder (8 cyl. model).
6 cyl. model (25·4 h.p., £19.10s. tax, 20 m.p.g., 80 m.p.h.). Complete £458
8 cyl. model (30 h.p., £22.10s. tax, 85-90 m.p.h.). Complete £558
STUDEBAKER DISTRIBUTORS LTD., 155-157 GT. PORTLAND ST., W.1. (EUS. 4444)
There is a Studebaker agent in your district
STUDEBAKER SPECIAL COACHWORK BY SALMONS AND SONS

62C Studebaker

62D Studebaker

63A: **Terraplane Panel Delivery** was based on Hudson's Terraplane car chassis. A total of 111,342 vehicles were produced in Hudson's Detroit plants during this year. 8,058 of these were commercial vehicles. Hudson was one of the first American manufacturers to locate the battery in the engine compartment, making it more accessible.
63B: **Terraplane DeLuxe Six** Sedan Model 71 was popular in Great Britain and a survivor is shown here at a recent rally of the Pre-50 American Auto Club. In this year Hudson made the ash tray standard equipment and dropped the rumble seat option on Coupés. For 1938 Terraplane became Hudson Terraplane.
63C: **Willys-Overland Four** was completely restyled and had 100-in. wb chassis with various body options such as Sedan (shown), Coupé, Roadster and Tourer. The WW II Jeep's 'Go Devil' engine was developed from the power unit of these cars. In Australia the Willys was available with locally made Sedan body.

63B Terraplane

OVERLAND PACKAGE
FREIGHT SERVICE
FREE STORE DOOR DELIVERY
DETROIT
TRUCKING
CO.

63A Terraplane

63C Willys

# 1938

Following ever-increasing sales figures since the 1932 slump, 1938 was a shattering set-back, with production down by 40%. More than one million fewer cars found customers than in 1937 and truck and bus production was down by almost half. The number of motor dealers had been on the increase since 1932 but towards the year's end had fallen again sharply. At the end of the year, however, business picked up again. Chevrolet's sales to dealers were down from 1,189,016 to 694,039 units. Chrysler put it like this: 'Sales and earnings for the year 1938 reflected the fact that business generally suffered a precipitate decline from the preceeding three years'. The Corporation produced only 570,852 units (less than half the 1937 output) but spent $18 million on improving its facilities, including the completion of a new truck plant. Chrysler also introduced a fluid coupling which 'eliminated all metal-to-metal contact between the engine and driving wheels'. Ford spent $40 million for plant expansion and introduced the Mercury. Several car makers, including Buick, Cadillac and Pontiac introduced steering column-mounted gear shift lever (1939 models).

GHK 723
64B Buick

64A Buick

64C Cadillac

GPL 314
64D Cadillac

64A: **Buick Eight Series 60 Century** Sport Coupé, Model 66S, had 'Opera Seat' in rear of passenger compartment. 'Dynaflash' valve-in-head engine produced 141 bhp.
64B: **Buick Eight CO Series** Convertible Coupé of Canadian origin. Buick's 1938 range with four Series was much the same as 1937 but grilles had fewer bars.
64C: **Cadillac Series 65 V8** Touring Sedan. 1938 range comprised Series 60 (124-in. wb), 60S (126-in. wb), 65 (132-in. wb) and 75 (141-in. wb) as well as V16 Series 90.
64D: **Cadillac V8** with standard Coupé bodywork by Fisher. The V12 was discontinued. A total of 24,950 Cadillacs and LaSalles were sold in 1938 (46,153 in 1937).

65A: **Cadillac Series 90 V16** was the most expensive model and sold at well over $5000. Cadillac was first with 135° V-type 16-cylinder engine.
65B: **Chevrolet Master DeLuxe Series HA** Town Sedan. The Master HB was a less luxurious version with rigid front axle. Series 018 Master Taxicab was also available.
65C: **Chrysler Royal Six** Sedan with 119-in. wb. Also available as 136-in. wb Seven-Place Sedan or Limousine. Larger Chryslers were the Imperial and Custom Imperial Eights.
65D: **DeSoto Six** came in two basic variants: S5 (119-or 136-in. wb) and SP5 (export, 112-in. wb).
65E: **DeSoto S5 Custom Six** resembled Chrysler Royal and Dodge in many respects.

FVX 660
65C Chrysler

65A Cadillac

65D DeSoto

65B Chevrolet

65E DeSoto

66A: **Dodge D8 DeLuxe Six** Convertible Coupé was one of ten models available in this 3·5-litre range. Wheelbase 115 and 132 in.
66B: **Dodge D8 Custom Six** Sedan. A smaller model, the D9 with 112-in. wb, was available for export. Treasury rating 25·35 and 19·8 HP respectively.
66C: **Fargo FJ1 Six** light truck chassis with 9·00 × 13 'desert tyres', one of more than 1000 delivered to Egypt. Incorporated many car components. Wheelbase 116 in.
66D: **Ford V8 Model 81A Standard 85HP** and **Model 82A 60HP** had 1937 style bodywork with revised grille. Wheelbase was 112 in. Tudor Sedan (700C) shown.
66E: **Ford V8 Model 81A DeLuxe 85 HP** with elegant Convertible bodywork made in Germany. Also available in the Netherlands. Note rear wheel shields.
66F: **Ford V8 Model 81A DeLuxe 85HP** Convertible Coupé (706A). 85 HP was also referred to as 90HP in Ford literature. In UK it was the '30HP'

---

EYW 791
66A Dodge

66B Dodge

66C Fargo

66D Ford

66E Ford

66F Ford

67A: **Graham Super Custom 120 Six** Four-door Sedan with the front wings modified to take later type lamps. Without running boards and bumpers this car was still in use in Czechoslovakia thirty years afterwards.
67B: **Hudson Terraplane Six** Sedan with 117-in. wb and L-head (side valve) engine of 16·9 HP (2723 cc) or 21·6 HP (3475 cc) RAC rating.
67C: **Hudson Terraplane Six** DeLuxe Convertible Brougham. With a 6·25:1 compression ratio the power unit developed 101 bhp. Wheelbase 117 in.
67D: **Hudson 112 Six** was new low-priced series introduced early in 1938 and mounted on a wheelbase of 112 in.
67E: **LaSalle Series 50 V8** Covertible Coupé looked like Cadillac but had narrower radiator grille. Wheelbase measured 124 in. Bodywork by Fisher.

67A Graham

BOW 337

67B Hudson

67C Hudson

L-2798

67D Hudson

67E LaSalle

Lincoln-Zephyr V-12
Knowing the Virtue of Multi-Cylinder Design, You May Have Wished You Could Afford a V-12. *Are You Sure You Cannot?* Don't be Too Positive Before You Have Tried THE LATEST LINCOLN-ZEPHYR V-12, demonstrably the last word in excellence of performance, in every way, coupled with economy—of purchase, running and maintenance alike.
Pioneer motorists all over the British Isles, automobile engineers who have studied every phase and development of motor design for thirty to forty years, are amazed, confounded, yet tickled almost to death, when they use a Lincoln-Zephyr V-12 for the first time. Riding in it is a revelation—driving it is getting an entirely new conception of motoring.
And yet . . . And yet Lincoln-Zephyr V-12 motoring costs so surprisingly little, although the more you get of it the more you want!
Catalogue for a postcard. Road-trial for a telephone-call. If there is not a Lincoln-Zephyr V-12 Distributor in your district, we are delighted to send a car to your door, in charge of a representative content to let it speak for itself.
May we send you also particulars of the Lincoln V-12, the most perfect, stately motor-carriage extant?
The Autocar
of February 25 last reported "Approximate normal fuel-consumption, 15-19 m.p.g."
COUPÉ · £525
FOUR-DOOR SALOON £550
LIMOUSINE · £610
CONVERTIBLE COUPÉ £645
CONVERTIBLE SALOON £675
LINCOLN CARS LIMITED
SOLE CONCESSIONAIRES IN GREAT BRITAIN FOR LINCOLN AND LINCOLN-ZEPHYR CARS
Great West Road, Brentford, Middlesex · Telephones Ealing 4506 · 4507 · 4508

68A Lincoln

68B Lincoln

68A: **Lincoln Zephyr 86H V12** was available in Britain with five body styles, namely Coupé, Sedan, Limousine, Convertible Coupé and Convertible Sedan. Treasury HP rating was 36·3.
68B: **Lincoln Zephyr 86H V12** differed from preceding model HB mainly in that the front end was completely restyled. Wheel- and springbase were increased by 3 in.
68C: **Oldsmobile L38 Eight** Four-door Sedan had 4213-cc engine of 33·8 HP (RAC). This rhd model sold in Britain at £515 (£415 for chassis only).
68D: **Oldsmobile F38 Six** Coupé with non-standard bumpers. Exterior difference between Six and Eight was in styling of radiator grille. Engine was 3764-cc (28·3 HP RAC).

DPO 367

68C Oldsmobile

68D Oldsmobile

69A: **Packard Super Eight, Sixteenth Series, Model 1603** Four-door Touring Sedan. The Super Eight was available with 127-, 134- and 139-in. wb lengths and with the exception of the 127-in. wb Sedan, body style availability was much the same as for the Twelve models. Less-expensive Packards were the Six 1600 (122-in. wb, prices ranging from just below $1000; five body styles) and the Eight 1601/1D/2 (127-, 139-, and 148-in. wb lengths, prices from $1225 up to $5100). Eight and Super Eight models included custom-built bodies by Brunn and Rollson.

69B: **Packard Twelve, Sixteenth Series, Model 1608** with Dutch custom-built convertible coachwork (Schutter & van Bakel, Amsterdam). These V12 models had a 175-bhp side-valve engine with $3\frac{7}{16} \times 4\frac{1}{4}$ in. bore and stroke. Taxable horsepower was 56·7 HP (AMA) Only 566 were produced from September 1937 until September 1938 and the factory offered fourteen body styles on chassis with 134 or 139 in. wb. Prices varied from $4135 for a Model 1607 2 + 2-seater Coupé with 134-in. wb to $8510 for either a Touring or All-Weather Cabriolet, both executed by Brunn on 139-in. wb chassis.

69A Packard

69B Packard

70A: **Plymouth P6 DeLuxe Six** Sedan had 113-in. wb and was also available as Business Six, with 112-in. wb. Engines: 3·3-litre (23·4 HP) or 2·8-litre (19·8 HP; export). UK nomenclature: Chrysler Kew.
70B: **Pontiac Silver Streak Six and Eight** were very similar in appearance. This is a Six (222·7-cu in.) Four-door Sedan with 117-in. wb. Eight had 122-in. wb.

70C: **Pontiac Six** Coupé was available as Business Coupé or Sports Coupé with so-called 'Opera Seats'. Except for Six Station Wagon, all models were also available as Eights (248·9 cu in.).
70D: **Pontiac** with a difference. This auto was customised and featured modified front and rear end, lockers in front wings, full instrumentation etc. Picture taken in England, 1967.

70A Plymouth

70B Pontiac

EXL 775
70C Pontiac

HXF 817
70D Pontiac

71A: **Studebaker** period advertisement of May 1938. Model ranges: Commander, State Commander and State President Eight. US prices (for Cruiser Sedans): $965, $1040 and $1205 respectively.
71B: **Studebaker State Commander Six** featured vacuum-actuated gearshift (control on dashboard), freewheel transmission and automatic hillholder as standard equipment. Commander models had conventional (round) headlamps.
71C: **Willys-Overland** was one of the smallest US cars and many of the year's production total of 26,673 were exported. Engine was economical 2·2-litre L-head.

CHOOSE YOUR CAR AS CAREFULLY AS YOU CHOOSE YOUR HOME
If you require your car to reflect the same good taste as your home—and it should; if you require it to provide the same restfulness—and it must; or if you look upon it as a lasting investment in quality—your complete answer lies in the inimitable Studebaker. Here is cradled comfort born of wider seating and unequalled suspension; styling as modern as the moment, yet as tasteful and practical as artist-engineering can make it. Here, too, are many unusual refinements—such as the Automatic Hill Holder and the Remote Control gear change—two important Studebaker "firsts" among 50 outstanding new features. And what is more, here is brilliant performance—engine power so flexible—so silently obedient that for all the driving effort it takes you might still be sitting at home. The more critical you are, the more reason you should own a Studebaker. Arrange a trial run to-day. (Name and address of your nearest agent gladly supplied on request.) Studebaker Distributors Ltd., 155-7 Great Portland Street, London, W.1. Euston 4444.
Studebaker

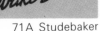

71A Studebaker

71B Studebaker

71C Willys

This year saw several US automotive milestones. Ford produced its 27 millionth vehicle, Chevrolet its 15 millionth and the nation its 75 millionth. Car and truck/bus production rose to 2,866,796 and 710,496 respectively. Buick now offered 30 models from $894 to $2453 and introduced a sunshine roof. Chrysler was closed down for 54 days by a strike but nevertheless had the fourth best year in its history thus far. Hudson introduced 'Airfoam' seat cushions, 'Autopoise' control, helping to keep the front wheels automatically on true course, and front-hinged hood with lock release under the dashboard. Nash built its 100,000th car with 'Conditioned Air Unit'. Oldsmobile increased sales volume by more than 37% and later in the year announced the first 'Hydra-Matic' fully-automatic transmission (in 1937 Buick and Olds had introduced an automatic gear changer called 'Automatic Safety Transmission'; this system used brake bands and plate clutches but had no fluid coupling and was not available for export). Packard, in addition to turning out 76,366 cars, designed, developed and produced a high-speed marine engine for the US Navy. Studebaker introduced its new low-price Champion which was an important factor in their 117% increase in the year's unit sales. Practically all US cars now had the gear shift lever on the steering column, either as standard or as optional equipment. The electrically actuated Borg-Warner Overdrive (with 'Kick down') also made its appearance.

72A Buick

72B Buick

72C Cadillac

72A: **Buick Eight Series 40 Special** Sport Coupé (with 'opera seats') Model 46S. This was Buick's cheapest offering, at $894. Wheelbase was 120 in., weight 3583 lb.
72B: **Buick Eight Series 60 Century** Touring Sedan with Trunk Back, Model 61. Again there were four Series: 40 Special, 60 Century, 80 Roadmaster, 90 Limited.
72C: **Cadillac Series 75 V8** Convertible Coupé had 141-in. wb. Other V8s: 61 with 126-in. and 60 with 127-in. wb. Series 90 was V16 in $5000 bracket.
72D: **Cadillac Series 60 V8** Sedan. Price in UK £850. This year Cadillac claimed: 'more than half of all fine (US) cars sold above $2000 are Cadillacs'.
72E: **Cadillac Series 75 V8** Fleetwood Limousine sold in Great Britain (with right-hand drive) at £1245 and had 5676-cc engine of 39·2 HP (RAC). Tyres 7·50 × 16.

72D Cadillac

FLX 5

72E Cadillac

**Chevrolet 1939** came in two series, the **Master DeLuxe Series JA** and the **Master 85 Series JB,** both with 85-bhp 3·5-litre engine. The Master DeLuxe was the first Chevrolet with 'Knee Action' ifs with open (exposed) coil springs and was very popular. Vacuum-assisted steering column gear shift was optional at $20 extra. The Master 85 had a rigid front axle. Shown:
73A: Station Wagon with Midstates Body Corp. bodywork, available on JA and JB chassis ($883 and $848 respectively).
73B: Imperial seven-passenger model, produced by GM in Antwerp had 134-in. wb, divided prop shaft, $\frac{1}{2}$-ton truck rear axle, 6·25 × 16 tyres.
73C: Period advertisement of Canadian-built Chevrolets. Prices: JA from £330, JB from £279.
73D: Sport Coupé, seating 2+2. Wheelbase of all models (except Imperial) was 112$\frac{1}{4}$ in.
73E: Master DeLuxe Sport Sedan had built-in trunk.
73F: Master 85 Coupé with (removable) Pickup box.

73A Chevrolet

73B Chevrolet

CHEVROLET 1939
30
OUTSTANDING FEATURES . . .
THE ENGINE.
6 cyl. overhead valve engine.
85 Brake Horsepower.
Octane Fuel Selector.
"Blue-Flame" Combustion Chamber.
Plated Iron Pistons.
Four-way oiling.
Crankcase ventilation.
Nozzle-spray valve-seat cooling.
Live rubber engine mounting.
TRANSMISSION.
★ Remote gear control.
Synchro-mesh gears.
Tiptoe-matic clutch.
COOLING SYSTEM.
Copper-core radiator.
Thermostatic control.
Leakproof pump.
Silent Fan.
SUSPENSION, STEERING AND SPRINGING.
★ Independent Frontwheel Suspension.
★ Shockproof Steering.
BRAKES AND FRAMES.
Perfected Hydraulic 4-wheel brakes with brake-shoe equalisers.
Stabilised front-end design.
Box-girder frame.
Hypoid-gear rear axle.
BODY.
Silent all-steel body.
Solid steel turret top.
No-draught ventilation.
Large luggage and tool compartment.
Padded-top seat backs.
Safety doorhandles.
★ Illuminated ignition lock.
Spare wheel mounted in luggage compartment.
★ ON MASTER DE LUXE MODELS.
Sales-EXCEEDING ANY OTHER CAR
Economy-OVER 20 M.P.G. -70/80 M.P.H.
Value-PRICE FROM £279
AND ALL THESE LUXURY FEATURES
CHEVROLET cars are the most popular cars in the world because they give the greatest value for money.
CHEVROLET cars are the leading product of General Motors.
CHEVROLET cars have beauty, quality, economy, performance, safety, comfort and reliability.
GENERAL MOTORS LTD.,
West Bay Road, Southampton.
Telephone: 72401. Telegrams: Hampautoex
CHEVROLET · A PRODUCT OF GENERAL MOTORS
London Distributors: British & Colonial Motors Ltd., 140, Long Acre, W.C.1. Temple Bar 3588

73C Chevrolet

73D Chevrolet

TK-40-60

73E Chevrolet

73F Chevrolet

## 1939

74A: **Chrysler Imperial.** Part of a fleet of 260 fully equipped surgical units, mobile first-aid posts and ambulances supplied for use in Britain at the beginning of the war.

74B: **Chrysler Imperial Eight** had 5·3-litre L-head engine with 82·55 × 123·8 mm bore and stroke, wb 125 in. British Dodge D23 Custom Eight was virtually identical. Chrysler Custom Imperial had 144-in. wb.

74C: **DeSoto** offered DeLuxe SP7 and Custom S6 models with 114- and 119-in. wb respectively. Engine taxable HP ratings were 23·4 and 27·3 respectively. Shown is Custom S6 Sedan.

74D: **Dodge D11 Luxury Liner Six** had 117-in. wb and 217·8-cu in. 87-bhp engine. For export there were also the 114-in. wb D12 and D12X. HP ratings 25.3, 23·4 and 19·8 respectively.

SURGICAL UNIT
74A Chrysler

FXV 888
74B Chrysler

74C DeSoto

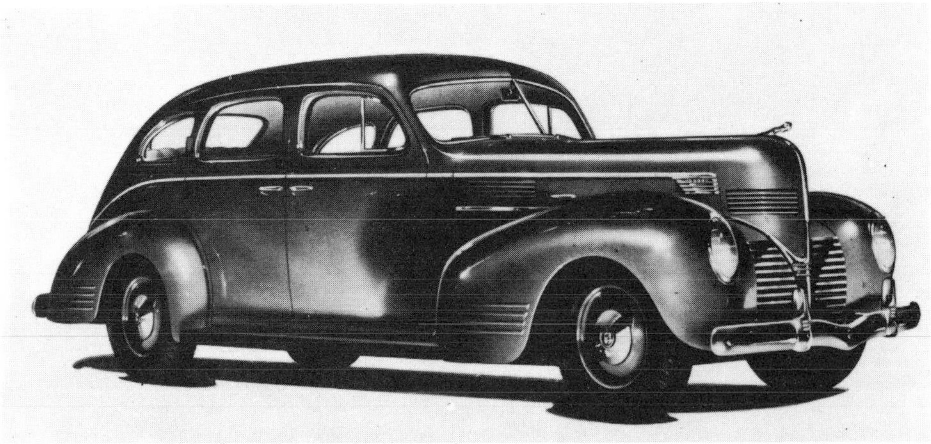
74D Dodge

75A: **Ford V8 Model 91A DeLuxe 85 HP** Convertible Coupé (Body Type 76). Other body options included Tudor (70B), Fordor (73B) and Convertible Fordor (74) Sedans, Coupé (77B) and Station Wagon (79).
75B: **Ford V8 Model 91A Standard 85 HP** and **Model 922A 60 HP** had same sheet metal as 1938 DeLuxe. Body styles included Sedans (70A, 73A), Coupé (77A), Sedan Delivery (78, shown), Wagon (78).

FXK 768

75A Ford

75B Ford

## EUROPEAN FORD V8s

75C: **British Model 62 2·2-litre,** produced 1936–39 (early models with spare wheel on back), then continued as 3·6-litre with military pattern front end.
75D: **French Matford F81 3·6-litre (and F82 2·2-litre),** 1938–39. Preceding F72 and F76 looked like British 62 but had built-in headlamps and forward-opening front doors. 1946–48 2·2-litre Ford F472A was like F72 again but with divided windshield, heavier bumpers and column gearshift. 1937–40 Chenard et Walcker U17 also used the 3·6-litre V8.
75E: **German Ford V8 3·6-litre,** 1938–39. Also in production was Model 92 with 2·2-litre engine. Various American types were produced in Cologne from about 1931.

75C Ford

75D Ford

75E Ford

## 1939

76A: **Hudson One-Twelve Six** Touring Brougham. This 112-in. wb series (various body options) was priced to compete with 'Big Three' offerings. Larger Hudsons had built-in headlamps.
76B: **La Salle Series 50 V8** Two-passenger Coupé was Cadillac's least expensive model. It had a 120-in. wb. The make was discontinued in 1940.
76C: **Lincoln Continental** Convertible and Coupé were first built in 1939 (as 1940 model) under the direction of the late Edsel Ford. Similar models were made in 1940–41 and 1946–48.
76D: **Lincoln Zephyr 96H V12** Sedan. 1939 models featured some styling changes including a new radiator grille with vertical bars, new bumpers, and other refinements.
76E: **Mercury 99 V8** was introduced by Ford in 1938 for the 1939 model year. This new make was aimed at the medium price field.

76A Hudson

76B LaSalle

76C Lincoln

76D Lincoln

76E Mercury

77A: **Nash Ambassador Six** Model 3925 Coupé, seating three, was built on a 121-in. wb chassis. **Ambassador Eight** had 125-in. wb, and same six body styles. Low-priced **LaFayette** models (10 body styles) had similar appearance but were less luxurious, on 117-in. wb.
77B: **Oldsmobile** 1939 models had 'Rhythmic Ride', an all-coil spring suspension combined with 4-way stabilisation and 'Knee Action' ifs, 'Observation type' bodies by Fisher (similar to Chevrolet and Pontiac) and 'Handi-Shift' steering column gear control. Shown is rhd Sedan.
77C: **Oldsmobile F39 Sixty** was new introduction in the low-price field. Other series: Seventy and Eighty. By late March over 100,000 1939 models had been produced (more than total 1938 model production). For 1940 models Hydra-Matic was first offered as optional extra.

77A Nash

KPC 643

77B Oldsmobile

JOHN F. IVORY

77C Oldsmobile

78A: **Packard Super Eight, Seventeenth Series, Model 1703** Four-door Touring Sedan (Body Type 1272) was offered at $1732 on 127-in. wb. Model 1705 had 148-in. wb.
78B: **Packard** Station Wagon with non-standard bodywork and some modifications to the lighting equipment, photographed in Spain. Cheapest 1939 model was Six (1700), priced from $888.
78C: **Plymouth** shared bodywork with other Chrysler Corp. products but all had distinguishing grilles and trim. Plymouth came in two series: P7 Roadking and P8 DeLuxe.

78A Packard

SP
B-216523

78B Packard

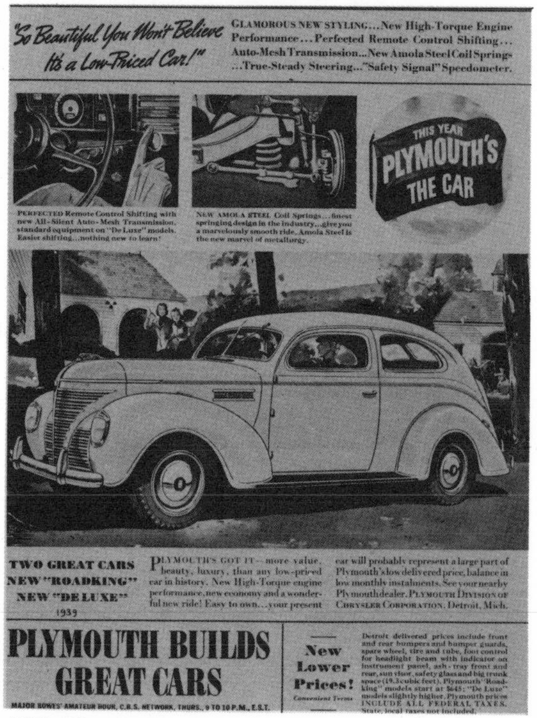
"So Beautiful You Won't Believe It's a Low-Priced Car!"
GLAMOROUS NEW STYLING...New High-Torque Engine Performance...Perfected Remote Control Shifting...Auto-Mesh Transmission...New Amola Steel Coil Springs...True-Steady Steering..."Safety Signal" Speedometer.
PERFECTED Remote Control Shifting with new All-Silent Auto-Mesh Transmission, standard equipment on "De Luxe" models. Easier shifting...nothing new to learn!
NEW AMOLA STEEL Coil Springs...finest springing design in the industry...give you a marvelously smooth ride. Amola Steel is the new marvel of metallurgy.
THIS YEAR PLYMOUTH'S THE CAR
TWO GREAT CARS
NEW "ROADKING"
NEW "DE LUXE"
1939
PLYMOUTH'S GOT IT—more value, beauty, luxury, than any low-priced car in history. New High-Torque engine performance, new economy and a wonderful new ride! Easy to own...your present car will probably represent a large part of Plymouth's low delivered price, balance in low monthly instalments. See your nearby Plymouth dealer. PLYMOUTH DIVISION OF CHRYSLER CORPORATION, Detroit, Mich.
PLYMOUTH BUILDS GREAT CARS
MAJOR BOWES' AMATEUR HOUR, C.B.S. NETWORK, THURS., 9 TO 10 P.M., E.S.T.
New Lower Prices!
Convenient Terms
Detroit delivered prices include front and rear bumpers and bumper guards, spare wheel, tire and tube, foot control for headlight beam with indicator on instrument panel, ash-tray front and rear, sun visor, safety glass and big trunk space (19.3 cubic feet). Plymouth "Roadking" models start at $645; "De Luxe" models slightly higher. Plymouth prices INCLUDE ALL FEDERAL TAXES. State, local taxes not included.

78C Plymouth

79A: **Pontiac DeLuxe 115 Six,** also known as 'Quality Six', had 115-in. wb. DeLuxe 120 Six and DeLuxe Eight had 120-in. wb. Six engine was 222·7-cu in., Eight 248·9-cu in., both L-head.
79B: **Studebaker Champion Six** was introduced in the spring as a new economical compact car. Custom and DeLuxe models were available with Coupé, Club Sedan (shown) and Cruising Sedan body styles.

79C: **Studebaker State President Eight** Club Sedan, like State Commander Six and Champion, was styled by Raymond Loewy. All models had independent front suspension with transversal leaf spring.
79D: **Willys-Overland** sold over 25,000 of its four-cylinder compact cars this year. In the annual Gilmore-Yosemite Economy Run they came first and second with over 26 mpg (US).

79A Pontiac

79C Studebaker

79B Studebaker

X-4423

79D Willys

## ABBREVIATIONS

| | |
|---|---|
| AMA | Automobile Manufacturers Association, Inc. |
| B×S | bore and stroke |
| bhp | brake horsepower |
| cc | cubic centimetre (=0·061 cu in.) |
| CKD | completely knocked down |
| CR | compression ratio |
| cu in. | cubic inch (=16·39 cc) |
| HP | horsepower, NACC, SAE and RAC; in Britain also known as treasury rating or taxable horsepower |
| ifs | independent front suspension |
| in. | inch (=2·54 cm) |
| L-head | engine with side valves |
| NACC | National Automobile Chamber of Commerce, Inc. |
| ohv | overhead valves (I-head) |
| qv | *quod vide* (which see) |
| RAC | Royal Automobile Club (GB) |
| SAE | Society of Automotive Engineers |
| sv | side valves (L-head) |
| wb | wheelbase |

## SUMMARY OF MAJOR AMERICAN CAR MAKES

### 1930–39 (WITH DATES OF THEIR EXISTENCE)

**CHRYSLER GROUP**

| | |
|---|---|
| Chrysler | (from 1923) |
| DeSoto | (1928-60) |
| Dodge | (from 1914) |
| Plymouth | (from 1928) |

**FORD GROUP**

| | |
|---|---|
| Ford | (from 1903) |
| Lincoln | (from 1920) |
| Mercury | (from 1938) |

**GENERAL MOTORS GROUP**

| | |
|---|---|
| Buick | (from 1903) |
| Cadillac | (from 1903) |
| Chevrolet | (from 1911) |
| LaSalle | (1927–40) |
| Marquette | (1929–31) |
| Oakland | (1907–31) |
| Oldsmobile | (from 1896) |
| Pontiac | (from 1926) |
| Viking | (1929–30) |

**HUDSON GROUP**

| | |
|---|---|
| Essex | (1918–32) |
| Hudson | (1909–57) |
| Terraplane | (1932–37) |

**NASH GROUP**

| | |
|---|---|
| LaFayette | (1934–36) |
| Nash | (1917–57) |

**NON-AFFILIATED MANUFACTURERS**

| | |
|---|---|
| American Austin/Bantam | (1930–41) |
| Auburn | (1900–37) |
| Continental | (1933–34) |
| Cord | (1929–37) |
| Crosley | (1939–52) |
| DeVaux | (1931–32) |
| Duesenberg | (1920–37) |
| Durant | (1921–32) |
| Erskine | (1926–30) |
| Franklin | (1901–34) |
| Graham (-Paige) | (1927–41) |
| Hupmobile | (1908–41) |
| Marmon | (1902–33) |
| Packard | (1899–1958) |
| Pierce-Arrow | (1901–38) |
| Reo | (1904–36) |
| Rockne | (1931–33) |
| Studebaker | (1902–66) |
| Stutz | (1911–35) |
| Willys (-Overland) | (1908–63) |

## ACKNOWLEDGEMENTS

This book was compiled and written largely from historic source material in the library of the Olyslager Organisation and in addition photographs and/or other material was kindly provided or loaned by the following:

American Motors Corporation, Chrysler Corporation, Ford Motor Company (USA, Great Britain and Germany), General Motors Corporation, General Motors Limited, Kaiser Jeep Corporation, *Old Motor*, and the Pre-50 American Auto Club, as well as the private collections of Jan Bakker, Fred van Leeuwen, Jan Polman and Bart H. Vanderveen. Thanks are also extended to Gerard W. Hitman and David J. Voller for valuable contributions and editorial comments.